Oregon Rivers

To Donna, Lloyd and
Erica —
Thanks for all
your help and support
in my project to protect
American rivers!

Tralie

Oregon Rivers

PHOTOGRAPHS BY LARRY N. OLSON

ESSAYS BY JOHN DANIEL

Larry N. Olson

FOREWORD BY DAVID R. BROWER

WESTCLIFFE PUBLISHERS

Englewood, Colorado

Designer: John Laursen
Production manager: Harlene Finn
Editor: Suzanne Venino
Oregon Rivers Map created by Interrain Pacific
Printed in Hong Kong by C & C Offset Printing Co., Ltd.

For more information about other fine books and calendars from Westcliffe Publishers, contact your local bookstore or write, call, or fax for our free catalogue:

Westcliffe Publishers, Inc.
2650 South Zuni Street
Englewood, Colorado 80110
(303) 935-0900 (telephone)
(303) 935-0903 (fax)

Limited edition prints of the photographs in this book, hand-printed and signed by the photographer, are available. Address inquiries concerning the photographs to:

Larry N. Olson
228 Furnace Street
Lake Oswego, Oregon 97034
(503) 635-5288

Library of Congress Cataloging-in-Publication Data

Daniel, John, 1948–
    Oregon rivers / photography by Larry N. Olson ; text by John Daniel
      p.   cm.
    ISBN 1-56579-229-7
      1. Rivers—Oregon—Pictorial works. 2. Oregon—Description and travel.
    3. Stream ecology—Oregon.   I. Olson, Larry N., 1951– .   II. Title.
    F882.A17D36   1997   97-8933
    551.48'3'09795—dc21   CIP

This book is dedicated
to the individuals and organizations
who care about Oregon's rivers and work to protect them.

FOREWORD

David R. Brower

There are many ways to salvation, and one of them is to follow a river. Way back in the Age of Engineers, when the Bureau of Reclamation proposed two dams in Dinosaur National Monument, a good many people like you climbed into rubber boats, bounced and glided down the Yampa River and the Green, and then howled so loud about what would be lost that Congress had to listen. Those dams were never built.

The story of Glen Canyon had a sadder ending, at least temporarily. Not enough of us knew that place, and so today 160 miles of the Colorado River's master sculpture work lie drowned behind an unnecessary dam, beneath a lake whose most significant function has been to evaporate water in a region where water is scarce.

The Age of Engineers is waning. I'm enough of an optimist to believe that before long, if we howl loud enough, that dam's two diversion tunnels will open, and the Colorado River will run free again through Glen Canyon, for the rest of time. (The dam itself can stay where it is. Passers-by, centuries from now, will wonder how humankind ever built it, and why.)

The better way is to protect wild rivers from needless dams and other improvements in the first place. I see from this book that Oregonians have been doing a good job of that. You're rich with rivers. Some of them I know, and these photographs have shown me many others—many portraits of water's wildness and a fine variety of landscape sculpture, Northwest-style.

You don't need it, but will you take some advice from a Californian who's been around a while? Cherish these rivers. Witness for them. Enjoy their unimprovable purpose as you sense it, and let those rivers that you never visit comfort you with the assurance that they are there, doing wonderfully what they have always done.

Keep your rivers flowing as they will, and you will continue to know the most important of all freedoms—the boundless scope of the human mind to contemplate wonders, and to begin to understand their meaning.

PREFACE

Oregon's rivers are as diverse as the state's climate and terrain. Each river has a unique character, its own flowing soul. The fifty-six photographed for this book represent our least disturbed watersheds, enjoying protection by law through inclusion in the National Wild and Scenic Rivers System and the Oregon Scenic Waterways System.

Larry Olson spent eight years seeking out the protected portion of each river, making repeat visits to many, searching for the right place in the right light. Each photograph is captioned with a few of his thoughts on the moment, the land, the river.

Sections of photographs alternate with essays by John Daniel. The essays sketch some of the geo-logical and ecological workings of rivers, their role in the human history of Oregon, and the spiritual significance of rivers through the ages.

Oregon has been in the forefront of river conservation nationally, and we can be proud of the measures taken to safeguard these fifty-six. Yet all our rivers, including many stretches of the ones pictured here, face ongoing threats to their beauty and natural integrity.

We offer these photographs and essays not as a guidebook or comprehensive catalogue, but as an array of glimpses, a celebration of the living waters of our state—the rivers we have, the rivers we still could lose.

Contents

OREGON'S WILD AND SCENIC RIVERS

These are the fifty-six Oregon rivers and river segments presently included in the National Wild and Scenic Rivers System and the Oregon Scenic Waterways System. The name of each river is followed first by the number of its location on the map, and second by the page on which its photograph is found.

A Map of the Rivers

Map created by Interrain Pacific. Data source: the Interior Columbia Basin Ecosystem Management Project.

BEGINNINGS

The canyon is a vault of light, its streaked volcanic walls rising hundreds of feet above me. A prodigious job of excavation for a river as small and mild as this one, the West Little Owyhee, flowing at its October low among yellow and russet willows. An overhang of stone is reflected in the clear moving water, and water is reflected on the stone—a rippling, wavering river of light follows the river that follows the stone. The stream sings a subdued music, a scarcely audible lilt, faint and fluid syllables not quite said. It slips away into its future, where it already is, and flows steadily forth from up the canyon, a fountaining of rumors from regions known to it and not to me.

We don't tend to ask where a lake comes from. It lies before us, contained and complete, tantalizing in its depth but not its origin. A river is a different kind of mystery, a mystery of distance and becoming, a mystery of source. Touch its fluent body and you touch far places. You touch a story that must end somewhere but cannot stop telling itself, a story that is always just beginning.

The West Little Owyhee starts somewhere in the vast sagebrush tablelands of far southeastern Oregon, maybe in a pocket of aspens dropping leaves into a pool, and the pool stirs, trickling over stones. Stories begin that way throughout the high desert country, on Steens Mountain and Hart Mountain, in the Trout Creeks and the Ochocos. And they begin, too, in dry rocky creases that wander the immense land as if lost. They are not lost. When snow melts or enough rain falls they are the rivers gathering, finding their way, forming themselves as they gradually form the land.

In the Cascades and the Coast Range, the Wallowas and the Strawberries, there are other kinds of beginnings. Spotting the forests are seeps and springs where grasses, mosses, and horsetails silently riot, growing and dying to grow and die and grow again. There are lakes surrounded by conifers or alpine meadow, lakes brimming full and overfull, pouring off through little ravines checked with boulders and the trunks of trees and beaver dams. Higher on the peaks there are slumping snowfields littered with rockfall, tinged pink with algae, the rubble below them glistening with melt. There are slow rivers of ice that hoard the story for centuries before letting it go in minuscule drops, in streamings milky with ground stone.

Start at any of those sources, let water lead you, and eventually you will stand where a river empties into the Pacific or a desert lake. The story isn't hard to follow. But start at the mouth and trace the story back, and your journey may involve more questions. Trace the Rogue River, to choose one. From its outlet at Gold Beach on the southern coast, follow it back through its wild canyon in the Klamath Mountains, through its broad valley between Grants Pass and Medford, and up past Lost Creek Reservoir into the Cascades. Climb alongside through the volcanic landscape, where at one point the river hurls itself into a lava tube and churns out of sight for two hundred feet. Follow still higher, until the Rogue is nothing but a creek joined by other creeks, all issuing from mountain springs, all small and white and fast. You could follow any of them. *Here*, says the river, *here* and *here*.

Stay with the blue line your map calls the Rogue and you'll arrive, on foot, at a place called Boundary Springs, high in the northwest corner of Crater Lake National Park. But even here you'll face choices. There are several springs, each of them bright with moss and rushing water. Where is the Rogue River now? The largest spring? Take off your boots, douse your feet. Watch how lucid water springs forth among shaggy stones and cascades lightly away. Watch how it flows. It does not gather and then begin to move. It is born in motion, a gesture already underway. This spring is only the place

where a river emerges from the deep cold joints of an exploded mountain, a subterranean wilderness fed by seepings out of Crater Lake, which itself is fed by underground springs, which themselves are fed by snowmelt sinking into soil.

Snowfall, then, is the source of the Rogue. But snow is only an expression of winter storms, and the storms are swirling eddies of a vast air mass that flows out of Siberia, soaks up moisture south of the Aleutians, and delivers barrages of weather to our West Coast. It is known as the Pacific maritime polar airstream, one of seven such atmospheric tendencies that shape the North American climate. The headwaters of the Rogue, the headwaters of every stream on Earth, is a river in the sky.

No one in the ancient world would have been surprised at such an idea, but the ancients knew their rivers in the sky through myth, not atmospheric science. The early Greeks imagined a divine river in the god Oceanus, who encircled the universe and coupled with his wife and sister, Tethys, to produce the three thousand earthly rivers. The Egyptians believed that not one but two Niles flowed through their cosmos—the great river of water whose floods fertilized their fields, and a celestial Nile that rose from the same source and tended across the heavens. By day it bore the boat of Ra the Sun; at night it was visible as the Milky Way. As civilization evolved in the Ganges Valley of India, it was believed that a heavenly river identified with the goddess Shakti poured down upon the head of Shiva, who eased the torrential power of her waters and sent them streaming to the four directions. The southern branch became the Ganges, which to Hindus is not only sacred but is divinity itself in liquid manifestation. Bathing in the Ganges, polluted as it may be, purifies one's present life—and past lives—of sin; pilgrims take home bottles of its water for healing.

The Book of Genesis gives a brief glimpse of that same archetypal river: "And a river went out of Eden to water the garden; and from thence it was parted, and became into four heads." Ezekiel envisions the waters of life as a small trickle issuing from the threshold of the Jerusalem Temple. As the Lord leads him downstream, the waters rise to his ankles, his knees, his loins, and finally they swell into a mighty river lined on both its banks with fruitful and medicinal trees.

Almost all mythic cosmogonies begin with water. It is the primeval element, "the face of the deep," the formless potentiality that pre-exists the created world and sustains its being. "Water flows," wrote religious historian Mircea Eliade, "it inspires, it heals, it prophesies. By their very nature, spring and river display power, life, perpetual renewal; they *are* and they are *alive*."

In Greek mythology the splash and stir of water came to be personified in the nymphs, female divinities of birth and fertility who cured the sick and raised mortal children to be heroes. Nymphs remained forever young and beautiful. They were sometimes oracles, and oracles in general were associated with springs and streams—maybe because of the inherent mystery in water issuing from the earth, or because water in motion sometimes seems to utter an elusive speech. Before responding to questions, oracles drank from the waters, often in a cave. Through them the mystery of living water expressed itself to the minds of men.

But like the oracle's news, the gifts of water were not always good. An ancient Syrian statue of the Great Mother shows her gowned in a river flowing from a vase she holds, fish swimming upward in its current. But the goddess appears in other images with demonic eyes, lightning jagging from her brow. On the Nile, the Indus, the Tigris and Euphrates, the giver of life was sometimes a destroyer, withholding her fertility and canceling human lives through drought or flood. Even the nurturing nymphs were feared by the Greeks as thieves of children, and in the midday heat they were capable of dissolving mortals in madness and drawing them to doom in the rushing waters. Through such images the ancients acknowledged that water is a wild power, ungovernable, containable only by paradox. Its nature is to give birth and to ruin, to sustain the things of creation and claim them to itself again.

That dual nature is central to the rite of baptism, which is at once a death—a disintegration of one's old identity—and a birth, a pouring forth of the divine into one's mortal life. It was originally a ritual not simply of water but of flowing water, water in its living movement. In Egypt, purification by water was associated with Osiris and Isis, god and goddess of the rising and falling Nile. In Hindu tradition, water must be set in motion by pouring from a vessel when no stream or river is available. Among Jews before the time of Christ, baptism was accomplished by immersing the naked boy in a flowing stream seven days after circumcision. Ritual pools were used as well, but John the Baptist shunned those and performed his baptisms in the

River Jordan, long known for its healing power. It was in the Jordan that John baptized the one who came after him—and when Jesus emerged from the river's current, "he saw the Spirit of God descending like a dove, and lighting upon him."

Many early Christians continued to baptize in John's way, as did Gnostic peoples such as the Mandaeans of Iran and Iraq. "Be baptized with the flowing water I have brought you from the world of light," it is written in their *Right Ginza*. "Clothe yourselves in white, to be like the mystery of this flowing water." In the modern world, pouring of water from a baptismal font or dunking in a pool are more common than immersion in a stream, but the symbolism of baptism remains powerful. Living water is the gesture from beyond. It returns us to beginnings and makes us anew. It joins the timeless to the temporal, the sacred to the secular, the heavenly to the mundane.

But if flowing water is a thoroughfare between those realms, it is also, ever paradoxical, the line of demarcation between them. Perhaps because rivers, aside from seashores, form the clearest boundaries to be found in nature, the crossing of a river is the human psyche's primary symbol for the passage of death. Beyond the earthly Jordan lies the promised land; beyond the spiritual Jordan lies the promised land of heaven. The Greeks buried their dead with a coin in the mouth for Charon, the grumpy boatman who ferried souls across the River Acheron to the realms of Hades. The Babylonians had a similar notion, and the theme occurs in both the Shinto and Buddhist traditions of Japan. (One of the ancient meanings of nirvana is "the far shore.") Among Hindus, holy sites are known as *tirthas*—fords—

because they are considered propitious places to make the crossing from this earthly world of illusion. It was inevitable that Herman Hesse's Siddhartha should come to a river near the end of his life of seeking. He lived out his days as a ferryman, poling travelers on their necessary journeys as he meditated on the river, listened to its voices, and heard in it at last all laughter and all sorrow, the flowing wholeness he had yearned for all his life.

When we cross the Willamette on one of the bridges in Portland or Salem or Eugene, we don't see it as a mythic being. We don't toss handfuls of grass as a sacrifice, as do the Masai of East Africa when they cross their rivers. Looking down on the workaday river with its tugs and barges and dry docks, its riprapped banks, we aren't likely to think of it as sacred or alive, a gesture from another world. We aren't moved to perform baptisms in it. We of the modern world have sought other kinds of value in our rivers. We have subdued them and turned them into channels of commerce. We have diverted them to water our fields, loaded them with sewage, torn up their beds and banks for gold and gravel, blockaded them to control their floods and extract their energy, stripped and muddied their basins for timber and pasture, poisoned them with industrial wastes, and reduced their abounding runs of wild anadromous fish to fractional remnants.

We have treated rivers as convenient perpetual motion machines, mere volumes of dutiful water at our disposal, yet even our tightly harnessed industrial rivers still beckon us. Whatever we have done to them, a mystery still flows before us. We walk and rest beside them, gazing, listening. When the docile waters rise, we flock to see the wildness in them, the wrack and foam, the intent sweeping power. Despite the damage floods do, it reassures us in our depths to know, with Wordsworth, that "The river glideth at his own sweet will." All of us have touched and been touched by flowing water. Our ancestors have eaten and loved and raised children by rivers for as long as we have been human, and longer. We have known the music of living water for the entire evolutionary saga of our coming of age on Earth. "It seems to flow through my very bones," wrote Thoreau of a brook he knew. "What is it I hear but the pure waterfalls within me, in the circulation of my blood, the streams that fall into my heart?"

Spiritually we understand rivers far less well than the ancients did, but even in the rational light of our science, the creative and destructive nature of running water remains wonderful enough. We know that it began its work as soon as rains first fell and traveled the face of the young volcanic planet, and if not for continual tectonic uplift, it would long ago have erased the continents into a global sea. Through that tireless attrition, that primordial youthful energy, water carves out runnels, clefts, ravines, hollows, valleys, chasms, canyons—the intricate inworn branching of watersheds, the aging face of the land, the very places we know as home. And in that webwork of water, in and around and gathered together by its flexuous body, a labyrinthine ecology connects our human lives to the least and greatest of the lives around us, an ecology we are only beginning to fathom and are unlikely ever to understand in its wholeness.

And of course we are connected historically to rivers. They led us into the continent and eventually across it. They showed the way into the Oregon Country for Lewis and Clark, for trappers and missionaries, for the pioneers of the Oregon Trail. Columbia, McKenzie, Illinois, John Day, Sprague, Smith, Deschutes, Powder, Malheur, Rogue—you can hear the history in the names, you can glimpse the stories we have spun around Oregon's rivers. But listen to more: Klamath, Imnaha, Sycan, Umpqua, Elk, Salmon, Snake, Wenaha, Wallowa, Clackamas, Nestucca, Chewaucan. There are other and older histories here, interwoven with the flowing of rivers for thousands of years before Europeans set foot on American land. And there are hints in those names of a truth beyond history or human culture, hints of a primeval vitality, hints of original voices sounding in the land before any human being was alive to listen.

The subdued autumnal music of the West Little Owyhee, flowing now in starlight beside my camp, is one such voice. There are many more. The Snake, where this mild water is bound, surges through Hells Canyon with the power of the Rocky Mountains behind it. The two Indian Creeks on Steens Mountain tumble down aspen-flagged valleys to the Donner und Blitzen. The White River flings itself from Mount Hood's shoulders; the Metolius wends its stately way through ponderosa pines; the Chetco, rising in the rugged Kalmiopsis, incises steep-walled canyons down to the sea. The Oregon land is alive with water. Where we haven't restrained them, the rivers still sound, their fountains spring forth from the world of light, they pursue unhindered the blind and beautiful labor of time.

SQUAW CREEK
JULY 1992

Squaw Creek originates from alpine tributaries on Broken Top Mountain, in the Three Sisters Wilderness of the High Cascades. I made this photograph on the third trip, after failing to get proper exposures on the first two. The combination of sun, shade, and white water is extremely difficult because the contrast is so great. Wind created by the falling water kept the tree boughs swaying constantly, which meant additional lost exposures. I spent many hours here making this photograph.

The Lostine River
August 1996

High in the Wallowa Mountains, above the upper end of this canyon, is a granite shelf complete with what seems like a Japanese garden—stunted pines with a bonsai look, perfect graveled representations of bodies of water with stone islands, and many creeks and tarns. This image was made at dawn, looking down the forks of Lostine Canyon. The clouds produced a summer snowstorm that lasted about four hours.

THE NORTH FORK OF THE SMITH RIVER
MAY 1993

One of three wild and scenic rivers that flow through the Kalmiopsis Wilderness, the North Fork of the Smith is the least visited. Grassy benches above the river are scattered with oaks, while alders line the riparian zone. Across the river from my camp was a small waterfall; downstream, the tributary in the left foreground of this image rushed in over boulders. Springtime inspired me to make many photographs along this stretch of river, and this one of a confluence was my favorite.

The Illinois River
November 1989

Most people don't associate the Illinois with flat water, because it is notorious as a difficult Class IV wilderness river. I've run it many times with my kayak overloaded with cameras, tripod, and camping gear. It's a painstaking, awkward, yet necessary way to reach remote areas for photographing. I made this image of sedges and spiraea while hiking along the riparian zone. The high fog burning off provided exquisite light.

JOSEPH CREEK

MAY 1990

For most of the year Eastern Oregon is anything but lush, but in the spring, the green hills and cliffs are reminiscent of Hawaii. High in the Blue Mountains at 4,700 feet, this region receives quite a bit of moisture. I never saw another person in the five days I spent here, though I did come upon a rattlesnake—one of only two that I encountered in eight years of shooting for this book. This photograph was made as a storm cell moved past, and the sun, breaking through the clouds, began to light the nearer ridge. I like the drama of the dark background of rain.

THE CHETCO RIVER

JULY 1990

A mountainside of red and green quartzite collapsed here, burying the Chetco River for half a mile with swirled, colorful rubble. You can hop from boulder to boulder down this stretch, sometimes not even seeing the river underfoot, just hearing it burble through shoots and tunnels. Giant redwoods thrive in this pocket of Oregon, but they are not protected and are in danger of being cut. In contrast, California has protected its remaining redwoods on public lands.

Big Marsh Creek

August 1992

Big Marsh Creek resembles the Florida Everglades. In spring a vast sheet of water moves slowly downslope to a canyon that gathers it into a creek. By August the marsh becomes a patchwork of dry grassy areas threaded with several distinct channels.

The flatness of the terrain and the tall sedges make this a difficult spot to photograph without a view camera or an extra-wide lens to create depth of field. Having neither, I spent a few hours climbing standing dead trees, hoping to shoot downward. I hoisted my camera and tripod over my head, hooked the handle over a branch and climbed up to it, repeating the procedure to the top, where I tried to wedge the tripod among the branches. This proved to be a low percentage technique. Finally I retreated to the marsh and found an open vista.

After forty years of water diversions and cattle grazing, this wetland is being restored by the Forest Service to its natural state.

LITTLE INDIAN CREEK
SEPTEMBER 1996

Little Indian Creek, on the west slope of Steens Mountain, is one of several tributaries of the Donner und Blitzen River. Seen here at sunset from above the headwaters, small entrenched creeks meander exactly as large rivers do. This U-shaped valley was plowed by glaciers during the last Ice Age, which ended about eleven thousand years ago.

THE NESTUCCA RIVER
JULY 1990

The Nestucca, and its headwaters, Walker Creek, are the only protected rivers in the Coast Range between Astoria and Cape Blanco. The Nestucca provides outstanding anadromous fish habitat, some of the most important in Oregon. Though protected from development, it is not protected from the ill effects of clearcut logging. The topsoil runs off the slopes with every rain, silting the clear water. I photographed these wetlands at dawn as a thin fog dissipated. Daisies and pink foxglove filled the valley. Beyond the borders of this view is a thin buffer of skinny alders, and then clearcuts as far as you can see.

The West Little Owyhee River
October 1991

Nestled in the far southeastern corner of Oregon, near both the Idaho and Nevada borders, the West Little Owyhee is remote, high, and arid. The river is a small, intermittent stream, pooling in shallows and disappearing in the sand. Native bunch grass and sagebrush dominate the landscape, and willows cluster wherever there is water. Cattle get into much of the canyon, leaving generous evidence of their visits.

I first tried to get here in May, only to find the dirt roads as slippery as glare ice from a late snowfall. The locals call this slick mud "gumbo." I slid from one side of the road to the other, trying to stay out of the ditches. At Antelope Creek the road dropped down steeply. If I had driven any farther, I wouldn't have gotten out for weeks. In October I went back and found the roads dry. I hiked the canyon bottom and the rimrock all the first day, making many exposures. That night, around 3:00 AM, I was alarmed to discover that several inches of snow had fallen. I packed up camp and left, fearing that otherwise I'd be spending a long winter on the West Little Owyhee.

THE ROGUE RIVER
MAY 1993

The lower Rogue is one of the original twelve rivers designated under the federal Wild and Scenic Rivers Act of 1968. The Wild Rogue Wilderness augments the protection of the wild and scenic designation.

The Rogue River flows deep in a wooded canyon, a botanically rich and diverse ecosystem, a true paradise. The canyon is either wet and lush or arid and sparse, depending on whether you're looking at a north-facing or south-facing slope. Madrone trees, with red bark peeling from their smooth trunks, cluster on the southern exposures. Most people float the river in three days, but eight- to ten-day trips are easily filled with explorations of side canyons. Rainy weather like this isn't what you hope for, but it's very typical of the canyon in springtime.

WATER WAYS

Few of our mountains are native. The Blues and the Klamaths have been here longest, scraped onto the western flank of proto-North America from the back of an east-drifting tectonic plate about 120 million years ago. Catty-cornered now, a state apart, the two ranges then sat side by side near Idaho, two island clumps in the deep sea that was Oregon. Three-quarters of the state's land mass arrived the same way, in a series of immigrations from the near and far Pacific. The foundation of the Coast Range came last, a volcanic archipelago that slammed home twenty or thirty million years ago, adding fifty miles to the continent. Today, an instant later, the Juan de Fuca plate plunges one inch per year beneath the lighter North American plate, which scrapes from it a wedgelike welter of oceanic deposits—the Coast Range, rising on its western side as short rivers dissect it, and subsiding to the east, thereby forming the faulted inland trough of the Willamette Valley.

The subducting Juan de Fuca raises periodic seismic and volcanic fits. The Cascades were born in several such fits, mounds of ash and lava tilting up to the east as streams wore furrowed flowlines into them. Still farther east, the crust of Earth stretched tectonically, vastly increasing itself, faulting into valleys between block mountains. Seventeen million years ago, that movement gave vent to stupendous lava flows that may have spread as fast as thirty miles per hour, creating in the course of several million years one of the largest flood basalt provinces in the world, thousands of feet thick. As flow after flow poured through the wide gap that preceded the Columbia River Gorge, the Columbia persistently shifted its channel northward, cutting around each new blockage of basalt.

In Pleistocene times, beginning two million years ago, ice sheets covered the High Cascades, the Wallowas, Elkhorns, and Strawberries, carving peaks into rocky horns, plowing broad sloping valleys down Steens Mountain. Glaciers flowed where streams had flowed before them; when the ice receded, streams flowed again in the greater valleys. The ice withdrew most recently about fifteen thousand years ago, leaving vast lakes in the low-lands, small lakes in the mountains. A lake is usually one of two things: a puddle left by a river of ice, or a river of water temporarily dammed by a moraine or slide or lava flow. Neither kind lasts very long. In a geological film of Oregon, shot from the sky at one frame per century, lakes would be seen to come and go like transient spatters of rain. Rivers would shift their channels from side to side, their meanders traveling downstream, but they would largely persist, largely hold their courses. The present channel may be young; the drainage pattern is very old.

There was a Columbia River before there was a Cascade Range. As the mountains upwarped, the river cut down and kept pace. (The many falls on the Oregon side of the Columbia Gorge may be evidence that those streams couldn't keep pace with the river.) In a similar way, the Rogue and Umpqua have downcut through the rapid uplift of the Klamath Mountains and the Coast Range; of the rivers originating in the Cascades, only those two achieve a direct Oregon outlet to the sea. In Eastern Oregon, the main stem of the Owyhee has been flowing in its present channel for upwards of five million years, adjusting all the while to volcanic eruptions, the stretch and tilting of the lively crust. The Metolius predates Black Butte, the volcano under which it now seeps, emerging in three great springs at the butte's northern base. The Deschutes has been incising Columbia River basalts for four to five million years, downcutting two to three thousand feet in that time. More recent lavas, from the Newberry vents, filled its canyon—and those of the Crooked and the Metolius—eight hundred feet deep. The rivers reclaimed their canyons in a mere one million

years, eating into the cold stone, reducing it to lava islands and high streamside cliffs.

But rivers do die, of course. They dry up, they are interred beneath miles of lava, and sometimes they devour one another. The present Snake River is thought to be a young cannibal. One of its Pliocene headwater streams came from the vicinity of a tight oxbow the river now makes as it flows northward into Hells Canyon. An older and much larger river system tended southwesterly through the same area, ponding up in ancient Lake Idaho. As the Snake River plain tilted northward, the young Snake wore through a divide, drained the lake, and captured the greater river's current, suddenly adding hundreds of miles and the snows of Yellowstone to its watershed. The decapitated river was left to dry and fill, a geologic ghost.

The Pleistocene was an eventful epoch for the Northwest, particularly the period from fifteen to thirteen thousand years ago. Lake Missoula in western Montana rose to a depth of two thousand feet behind an ice sheet blockage that periodically gave way, releasing five hundred cubic miles of water at a time to surge across eastern Washington in a sixty-five-mile-per-hour flood. The deluge channeled into the Columbia at Wallula Gap, ponded up a thousand feet deep when it hit the narrows of the Columbia Gorge, then backed up again on the lower Columbia and inundated the Willamette Valley nearly to the present site of Eugene. The site of Portland was drowned four hundred feet deep. The valley lake may have persisted for weeks at a time, a muddy roil tossing icebergs and torn-out trees. Boulders from five hundred miles away were stranded around the valley, borne in by ice.

Those erratic boulders and other evidence of the floods, including Washington's great coulees and Montana gravels deposited high in the Columbia Gorge, made sense to no one except one geologist named J. Harlen Bretz, who announced the flood theory in 1923 and defended it for decades against a disbelieving profession. The clincher came when a series of long parallel hills in Montana were identified from an airplane as what they are: ripple marks left by the greatest floods in Earth's geologic record. There may have been forty or fifty of them. Among their many consequences are the rich Willamette silts, tens to hundreds of feet deep, that farmers plow today.

Over ninety-seven percent of the water on Earth is in the oceans. Ice caps and glaciers hold just upwards of two percent. Most of the slight remainder, six-tenths of one percent, occurs as groundwater, ranging from the top of the water table to a depth of three miles. A smidgen, seventeen one-thousandths of one percent, will be found in lakes. A smaller smidgen, one one-thousandth of one percent, circulates as vapor in the atmosphere, to an altitude of seven miles. By far the smallest fraction of the world's water, at any one moment only one ten-thousandth of one percent, occurs in rivers and streams. But without that tiny portion of water that flows, the face of the planet would be the face of a stranger.

In shaping the land we live in, not to mention our cultures and civilizations, water in motion is the most crucial of geologic processes. Strangely,

though, it has been generally recognized for only two centuries that water shapes the land at all. Aristotle, Leonardo, and others throughout history have understood erosion, but the prevailing view through the Middle Ages and even into the early nineteenth century held that valleys pre-existed their streams. They were thought to be effects of the Biblical flood or of natural catastrophe. Knowledge of the Ice Age floods in North America would have aided that view, had it been available, but landscape in the long run changes very gradually. Catastrophism released its hold on the human mind slowly, as stone gives way to a river.

And where did the water of streams and rivers come from? That mystery also persisted for centuries. The ancients could see that rain and snow augmented streams, but not enough fell, it seemed, to account for year-round flow. (If the ancients had lived in Western Oregon, they would have figured it out.) It was thought that the encircling river, Oceanus, penetrated underground and rose, purified of its salt, in springs and streams. Scientific understanding of the hydrologic cycle didn't come into general focus until the seventeenth century, when a Frenchman measured rainfall in the Seine basin and found it six times adequate to account for the river's discharge. It was left for the astronomer Edmund Halley to complete the cycle by identifying the origin of precipitation.

In the course of a year, a full three feet of water evaporates from the world's oceans. Nine-tenths of that falls directly back to its source; one-tenth falls on land as rain or snow. A molecule of that land precipitation that runs off into a stream is likely to be in the ocean again within a few days or weeks, or it may return to the atmosphere immediately through evaporation. Other routes are slower. The molecule may spend decades in a lake, centuries in a glacier. If it enters the soil, and isn't sucked into a plant and transpired, it might percolate through the semisaturated surface zone toward the nearest lake or river. Or it might descend to the water table, the zone of saturation in which every crack and pore is packed with water, and travel there an inch or two a day through aquifers of sand or gravel, of fractured or porous rock. If the molecule sinks deeper than half a mile, it is likely to meet rain that fell ten thousand years ago and will return to the hydrologic cycle only when a tectonic disturbance releases it. Deeper yet, hot from the radioactive decay of Earth's core and loaded with dissolved salts, lies water that left the cycle millions of years ago. And still deeper, bound up in crystalline rocks, there exists water that has never flowed—water that was present in the spinning dust from which the solar system formed.

But rivers care nothing for those deep places. Rivers are children of sky and upper Earth, deft and changeable children, born from rain and snowmelt fed into their channels by steady seepage from the zone of saturation. That seepage provides the river's base flow, its minimum year-round level. When rain swells the base flow, by percolation through the banks and surface runoff, there is an increase in the river's discharge, the volume of water per second passing a particular point. A river is a self-adjusting organism, and so any change in discharge must be answered by changes in other dimensions—mainly, channel width, channel depth, and velocity of flow. In small streams of upper drainage regions, increased discharge results primarily in higher velocity, with a smaller increase in channel depth. In lower regions, along the river's floodplain, discharge is inherently greater due to continual contributions of seepage and tributaries along the way, and the effects of storm contributions are magnified. This heightened discharge is accommodated by a downstream increase in channel width, a lesser increase in depth, and often—surprisingly—a higher velocity than occurs in the river's mountain origins.

How can a flatter stretch of river flow faster than a much steeper stretch? Because gradient is not the only determinant of velocity. The loss in gradient is more than compensated by the enlarged river's greater discharge, and by two factors that reduce frictional drag: the evenness of the downstream bed, which is typically more sandy than rocky, and the fact that as the river grows in volume, the portion of its flow in contact with the bed and banks grows proportionately smaller. High in the Cascades, the little Rogue River tumbles down steep slopes but tumbles inefficiently, squandering much of its energy as it dashes among rocks and fallen trees. Close to its mouth, two hundred miles downriver, it flows at a milder pitch but flows evenly, massively, with gathered and concerted power, along its smooth sandy bed.

But even that smoothest reach of river flows evenly only in a relative sense. A river never moves at uniform speed across a transect of its flow. In a smooth artificial channel, and perhaps for brief passages in very even natural channels, the current may exhibit laminar flow: the water glides in stable layers shearing one atop another. But the riverbeds of nature are variously irregular, creating complexity of movement. Water progresses downstream chaotically, with backflows and eddies, upflows and downflows, velocity pulsations, rollers, and standing waves. It is a continuous dance of turbulence, slackening only in a thin boundary layer near banks and bed, where velocity decreases to a theoretic zero.

Within that dance another dance is going on. A water molecule is an electrically dipolar structure, its two hydrogen atoms forming a positive pole and its oxygen atom a negative pole, causing the unbalanced molecules to attract each other like tiny magnets. This hydrogen bond, as it is known, makes water cling together at the molecular level in a cohesive continuity, bound more tightly than the molecules of some metals. As ice, the molecules are held in a set matrix; but in the fluid state, the hydrogen bonds loosen enough for the molecules to swirl liquidly in constant motion, small bands of them bonding and unbonding willy-nilly in an ongoing submicroscopic frolic. The upshot, to our senses, is a substance that can resist no stress and therefore cannot hold still, that is easily parted by anything solid but as easily rejoins itself and dances on.

When water wets soil or rock (or a water glass, for that matter), some of its molecules form hydrogen bonds with the molecular constituents of those solids. It is this capacity, together with the acids it carries, that makes water a nearly universal solvent and thus the powerful agent of weathering and erosion that it is. Physical force is also important: a wind-driven drop of rain actually blasts tiny shards out of rock of any hardness. The aggregate effect of those little explosions and dissolutions is the reduction of the North American continent by about one foot every ten thousand years. Water loosens it, bit by bit, and water bears it away. To earth scientists, a stream is not a dancer but a worker, and its work is the carrying of its load—a dissolved load of rock and soil constituents, a suspended load of sand and other small particulates, and a bed load of gravel and larger stones that roll and bounce and slide along the bottom during high flows.

Like width, depth, and velocity, a river's capacity to carry its load varies with discharge. Peak flow events can scour the channel deeper by several feet, then rebuild it as discharge drops and the current loses its capacity. Differential current speeds sort the load as it's released, commonly producing an alternating pattern of pools—deep areas of slow current bedded with fine particles—and riffles, shallow stretches of livelier current and a gravel-cobble bed. A riffle is both transient and permanent; its stones are replenished from upstream as they wash downstream, the structure staying in place. Riffles alternate side to side in the channel, and consistently, in streams of all sizes, they occur at a distance of five to seven channel-widths apart. No one knows why.

In a straight reach, a river's fastest flowline tends to run in the center of the stream, just below the surface (because the atmosphere exerts a minute friction), but in most rivers most of the time the fastest flowline will swing from bank to bank with the curving of the channel. As the current presses into the outside of a bend, it piles slightly from centrifugal force and plunges strongly downward, eroding the bank and bottom, then rises as it crosses the center of the channel to surge against the outer bank of the next bend. And so the river body as a whole spirals down its channel, a helical dynamo carving pools at its outside bends, depositing the eroded material in riffles and in bars along the inside bends.

Sinuosity is the lovely term for the windingness of rivers—or, if you prefer Greek to Latin, *meandering*. (The word comes from the river Maeander in Asia Minor, known anciently for its curving habit.) It used to be taught that meandering is characteristic of aged rivers, something like the aimlessness of a senile mind, and it is true that a lowland river in a broad valley will meander widely across its floodplain. But in fact all rivers meander, if permitted by their underlying geology. Straight reaches more than ten channel-widths in length are extremely rare, and even in a straight reach the deepest part of the channel will swing from side to side. Using laboratory flumes and various bed materials, researchers have watched sinuosity develop in a stream of constant discharge flowing in a perfectly straight channel. Local erosion gives the stream a small bed load, which it transports a short distance and deposits along the same bank it came from. Thus a slight bend is born, helical flow develops, and the initial bend propagates others downstream as the current deflects from bank to bank.

There is as yet no entirely satisfactory theory explaining why rivers meander, and the mystery is not limited to rivers. All flowing water is sinuous. Ocean currents, trickles over smooth stones, the raindrop coursing down your windshield. Water takes a winding way. Small streams wind small, big rivers wind big—mapped and brought into scale with each other, their sinuosity looks exactly the same. The wavelength of a river's meanders—the straight-line distance between the apex of one bend and the apex of the next similar bend—will almost always equal seven to ten river-widths. No one can account for this regularity. It seems to reflect a primary natural law, some original pact that water made with gravity and the solid matter of the world.

The ghostly mathematics of running water extends to the structure of watersheds, which tend to be dendritic, or treelike. Tributaries grow like branches, elongating at the tips and bifurcating as the drainage pattern impresses itself into the land. The twig-tips are categorized by geomorphologists as first-order streams—those with no tributaries. The stream formed by two first-order streams is second-order; two of those joining yield a third-order stream, and on up the ranks. (On the ground, a first-order stream is a creature hard to identify. Small permanent streams are fed by intermittent streams, which are fed by transient rills, which merge upslope with the planar landscape. In practice, a river's order depends on the scale of the map used to analyze the watershed. By one analysis, the Willamette is an eighth- or ninth-order river, and the Columbia is twelfth-order.)

In any dendritic watershed, a stream of a given order is very likely to have either three or four tributaries of the next lower order. A fifth-order stream, for example, will have three or four fourth-order tributaries, and each of those will be fed by three or four third-order tributaries, and so on. Further, each lower-order tributary will be about half the length of the higher-order stream it feeds, and each will drain about one-fifth the area drained by the larger stream. The network shapes itself in a proportionate pattern, and that pattern holds roughly true in watersheds at any scale, from the tiny tracks of rainwater on a sloping desert stone to the enormous drainage of the Amazon, the biggest on Earth.

A dendritic network is the most efficient means of draining a slope; it requires less total length of channel than would, say, a network of parallel, non-branching tributaries feeding a central channel. It can be predicted that a watershed will form dendritically, unless prevented by obdurate geology, but it can't be predicted exactly where the branching channels will form, how the pattern will arrange itself in any one case. The pattern occurs but is not imposed; it is formed by the very flow of energy and mass it organizes. Networks of roots or neurons or blood vessels develop the same way—the general pattern determined, the particular realization singular. Schematically, those networks are very hard to distinguish from the network of a watershed. The dendritic form seems to be an archetype, a habit of nature integral to the very being and becoming of things. When Thoreau wrote of waterfalls in the circulation of his blood, of streams flowing into his heart, his imagination touched a pattern that unites us deeply with the patterned world around us.

THE OWYHEE RIVER
MAY 1991

One hundred and ten miles of protected river—one of Oregon's longest designated stretches—the Owyhee flows between vertical walls of basalt more than a thousand feet high. The canyon is filled with fantastically eroded geologic features of red, ochre, buff, and chocolate volcanic ash sculpted by wind and rain.

A gloomy overcast had cut short the available light, and the day's photography appeared to be over. I was cooking my usual soup and noodles when unexpected rays of sun seeped through the clouds on the horizon. This narrow slot of warm light illuminated the cliffs, leaving the sky and foreground in shadow. I grabbed my tripod with the camera still mounted and ran up and down the bank, jumping sage and rabbitbrush, looking for the perfect vantage point. By the time I was satisfied with the perspective, I had just seconds to make two photographs before the light vanished. I couldn't believe what I'd seen, and could only hope that I had chosen the proper exposure.

The Deschutes River
April 1991

The springtime leaves on these willows and alders are yellow, reddish, or light green due to various pigments. In summer, dark green chlorophyll flushes the leaves, masking the underlying colors. I made this photograph in midmorning as the sun burned through an overcast sky. Before these few minutes of evaporating clouds, the light was dull and flat; afterward, it was too contrasty and washed out.

The Elk River

July 1990

Late in July, low water reveals river-sculpted bedrock. The lower canyon is narrow, heavily forested, and dark. The absence of direct light until midday extends the time available to make photographs in the softly lit shade, but I found it necessary to use a long exposure.

The Crooked River
May 1991

The fifteen protected miles of the Crooked River flow between towering cliffs like the ones seen here. The lichen-encrusted columns were formed when molten basalt cooled and crystallized.

In spring, a natural river system should be full. Much of the water in this river has been diverted for agriculture, to the detriment of its fish and waterfowl. Shallow water heats up quickly in the sun—another hardship for fish.

The Metolius River
May 1991

"Metolius" is the word Warm Springs Indians used for the native salmon that once were plentiful but now are extinct, blocked from their spawning waters by Pelton Dam on the Deschutes. The Metolius is a beautiful river with clear water that flows beneath Black Butte and emerges in huge springs. The few remaining old-growth ponderosas suggest what this watershed once looked like.

The North Fork of the Sprague River
May 1993

The North Fork of the Sprague flows across the northwest corner of the Gearhart Mountain Wilderness. The headwaters wind through open forest and meadows before descending into a spectacular basalt canyon. Winters are long at 6,000 feet—by May the snow had just melted, and these buttercups were already in bloom. Wild trout survive in this river.

The Salmon River
March 1993

The Salmon River originates high on the south slope of Mount Hood and pours through the Salmon-Huckleberry Wilderness, making a wide U-turn west and then north before dropping into the Sandy River. The wildest stretch contains an impassable gorge with many high waterfalls.

THE ROARING RIVER
NOVEMBER 1990

Spongy mosses and ferns envelop the bigleaf maples in this scene, typical of a Pacific Northwest temperate rain forest. A lovely grove of western red cedar and western hemlock form the backdrop. The Roaring River drainage is densely forested with hemlock and fir, mostly uncut. Remote and wild, the area surrounding the stream has been proposed as a wilderness.

WALDO LAKE

OCTOBER 1990

The only lake in the Oregon Scenic Waterways System, Waldo Lake is the headwaters of the North Fork of the Middle Fork of the Willamette River. The lake water is some of the purest in the world. Diamond Peak appears in the background to the left.

This October morning, a fresh dusting of snow had turned a seasonally busy destination into a serene, mysterious presence. I stepped lightly along the wooded shoreline, afraid I was making too much noise. For me, the first snowfall of the year is the most wonderful transformation in nature. Overnight, winter settles in; the other seasons approach so slowly you can't say exactly when one has arrived and the other departed.

The Clackamas River
November 1990

While searching for autumn color, I was lured to this narrow constriction with its vivid mosses. October had been very wet, and by the time this photograph was taken the rain had knocked the fragile fall leaves off most of the trees. The same rain had plumped up the mosses with new growth and color. In summer, during their dormant state, the mosses are dull and dried up.

Big Indian Creek
September 1990

This colossal gorge is one of the most spectacular on Steens Mountain. The rock, glowing here in the last few minutes before sunset, is reddish-brown basalt. Glacial cirques can be seen across the canyon. Small tarns or ponds are scattered below them.

LIFE AMONG THE RUINS

"Rivers," geologist Luna Leopold has written, "are gutters down which flow the ruins of continents." His definition is undeniable as far as it goes, but it only goes so far. A lot happens in those gutters, not all of which is geological. If rivers run with entropic inevitability, life in rivers constitutes an ongoing stay of the inevitable. The geologic river works most efficiently unchecked. The ecologic river checks the flow at every opportunity and takes advantage of every check, setting its creatures stubbornly in place with adaptive forms and behaviors, mounting an elaborate and ingenious resistance from within the very grasp of almighty gravity.

Sinuosity aids the biologic conspiracy. If rivers ran straight they would offer an inauspicious sameness of habitat, not to mention fiercer currents. Meanders generate pools, riffles, eddies, bars, a varied and shifting mosaic of bed materials and current speeds and sun exposures. The exploitation of those variances is canny and complete. Pools, for example, are erosional features par excellence—sites scooped out and scoured at high water, signs of the gutter working at its violent best. But those same pools, at lower water, are the stream's richest havens of life. A pool is a hedge against quick export of the organic material—leaves, needles, twigs, feces, dead organisms—that provides fuel for stream food webs. In a well-pooled stream, organic matter is released only after thorough processing reduces it to fine particles and dissolved carbon. Ecologic efficiency thrives on retention.

Pools are structures intrinsic to the geomorphology of streams, but they are also created by objects and forces from outside the stream. In Oregon watersheds before Euro-American settlement, great numbers of large trees fell into streams and rivers. Fallen trees structured much of the total channel length of streams up to fourth-order, yielding a characteristic stairstep pattern of flat pools behind debris dams and plunge pools below them. The fallen trees themselves became habitat and food for various invertebrates, including some of the longest-lived insects known to science, and the pools they formed were essential rearing sites for young trout and salmon, providing ample food and protection from swift currents.

In larger streams, fifth-order and higher, fallen trees rarely formed complete dams but did contribute to the formation of braided channel systems with bars and quiet backwaters where young fish and waterfowl could thrive. High flows shifted and reconfigured the wood debris, intricating the river into an ever-changing complexity of structure and habitat. As late as 1870 the Willamette River flowed in at least five channels between Eugene and Corvallis, its floodplain cloaked with half a mile of forest on each side. Over a ten-year period on one fifty-mile stretch of the river, more than five thousand drift trees were removed from the channel for reasons of commerce and recreation—trees up to nine feet in diameter and a hundred and twenty feet long.

Drift trees of that size and larger once entered the Pacific in droves, the normal attrition of healthy, rivered forests. Most of them stranded on the coast, but some caught a current and rafted westward, high seas emissaries from the old-growth watersheds of the Northwest. Much of the driftwood on the Hawaiian Islands derives from the west coast of North America. Ancient Hawaiian cultures prized Douglas fir above all, crafting it into double canoes that carried their chieftains. Along the way, trees and rafts of trees became nuclei of marine food webs involving plankton, small fish, tuna, and porpoises. And at least one animal species of Northwest streams, the humble water strider, became a North Pacific seafarer, living and propagating on the woody flotsam of its home forests.

This aboriginal mode of log export has drastically diminished in the last hundred years, as old-growth forests have been clearcut and river channels improved. And beaver dams, another principal means by which stream waters were detained—especially important east of the Cascades, where sparser forests contribute fewer debris dams—are also much rarer now. Those most industriously American of animals (European beaver don't build dams) once transformed waterways into stable strings of ponds verging into wetlands, wetlands that absorbed flood waters and released them slowly, keeping the water table high and springs flowing. Almost half a million beaver were trapped out of Oregon and southwest Washington during one four-year period in the 1830s; by 1900 the beaver was close to extinction in this region. As the dams washed out—the beaver repairs its construction nightly—streams began to run unchecked, incising their channels and separating themselves from their floodplains.

The genius of a floodplain is that it takes on storm flows and diffuses their power. Water rushing in the channel loses much of its energy when it overtops its banks, and riparian vegetation—willows, cottonwoods, various shrubs and herbs—further restrains it, filtering sediment and fertile biomass from the flow. A river is an equilibrium between channel and floodplain, erosion and deposition; a river that can't get to its floodplain can only erode. The characteristic look of the lower reaches of the Sprague, the Malheur, the John Day, and many other dryland streams—incised single channel, raw cutbanks, poor streamside vegetation—is the result of many impacts, including more than a century of grazing and logging. But their decline was set in motion before a single wagon had traveled the Oregon Trail, by traders of the North West and Hudson's Bay companies responding to a craze for black beaver top hats in the capitals of Europe.

By one estimate, Oregon's beaver population may stand at about one-tenth its ancestral level. In some regions of the state, including some heavily logged areas, they are coming back—beaver are fond of willow, young alder, and salmonberry, species that pioneer logged-over riparian zones— but their dams are relatively few, and dams formed by fallen trees are also far fewer than they were. Most watersheds in the Cascades and Coast Range have been stripped of sizable wood; their streams have lost their most important structural element. A recent re-survey of Columbia Basin streams first surveyed in the 1930s shows an average deep pool loss—outside of wilderness areas—of seventy-five percent. Fewer pools mean fewer fish, impoverished ecosystems. Unchecked flow means faster downcutting, more sediment movement. The streams still flow, and many of them still look beautiful, but the landscape loses its margin, its resilience, its capacity to absorb change. Slowly, and not so slowly, the landscape loses its life.

It's hard enough to make a living in a river under the best of circumstances. Most organisms manage by anchoring themselves to the bed material or obstructions in the channel. A boulder in the current forms an eddy on its downstream side, a refuge for various creatures, and its nooks and crevices and protected undersurface offer additional niches. Cobbles, gravel, even grains of sand provide exploitable substrates suited to different forms of life. Plants of all kinds are used for shelter as well as for food. And beneath the river's bed and banks, in the saturated zone where water moves downstream much more slowly, invertebrates that do not live in the channel can be found, some of them unpigmented and blind.

Most surfaces receiving light in a stream will be blanketed by tiny forests of periphyton, a diverse assemblage of algae, euglenoids, and bacteria that grows in crusted, stalked, filamentous, and gelatinous forms and varies through the seasons. Each population is adapted to the flow regime of its reach of river. Some species of algae, for instance, will grow erect in colonial forms in easy currents, prostrate and in crevices in faster water. Periphyton attaches to its substrate with specialized basal cells or glues itself with basal mucilage.

The periphyton mat is cropped by various grazing invertebrates. Snails often dominate the headwaters of Oregon streams, plowing through the miniature forests and scraping them up with raspy tongues. Black fly larvae graze for part of their life cycle, but also, taking advantage of the current they must resist, attach themselves to stones and filter fine particulate matter from the stream flow. The larva, anchored at its base, leans far back in the current with two feathery fans extending from its head, one sometimes held lower than the other to catch drift passing at different levels. Caddisfly larvae spin silky nets and make protective cases for themselves by embedding sand, pebbles, and bits of stick into a tube of silk. They are acutely adapted to nuances of current—one species will be found on a rock's upper surface in the fastest flow, another lower down in the intermediate zone, still another on sheltered undersurfaces.

Adaptive body forms and behaviors enable many creatures to stay put. The water-penny, a kind of beetle, looks like a completely flattened pill bug; it clings fast to stones with the help of tiny spines ringing its oval body. Tadpoles in rapid streams are equipped with a hydraulic sucker that allows them to hold on and crawl. (An ecologist reports that stones five times the tadpole's weight can be lifted using the tadpole as a handle.) Baetid mayfly nymphs have perfectly streamlined bodies, widest one-third of the way from the head; the long tapered abdomen swings freely like a weathervane, orienting the nymph directly into shifting micro-currents. Trout and salmon are shaped similarly, blunt in front and tapered behind, the form that best reduces turbulent drag created when an object separates the flow of current.

Salmon protect their eggs from current and predators by depositing them into gravel pits, called redds, the female makes by flapping her tail as she lies on her side. After the hovering male ejects his milt, the female excavates a new pit just upstream, the gravel she displaces covering the eggs just fertilized. Certain minnows take more extreme measures. They deposit eggs in a cleared pit, like salmon, but then the male heaps gravel over them in a pile as high as twelve inches and as wide as three feet, carrying the pebbles in his mouth. To create this structure, one three-inch minnow may swim a total distance of fifteen miles carrying an aggregate underwater weight of eighty-eight pounds.

Reduced to a mouthful, the story of animal life in a river is this: small ones cling to rocks and wood, big ones eat small ones who have lost their grip. Not surprisingly, there is a continuous background level of small organisms—mostly insects, crustaceans, and snails—flushed downstream at the mercy of the current. This phenomenon, known as the drift, may reflect accidental dislodgement in an environment that wants nothing to stay where it is. But for reasons not completely understood, the population of the drift jumps sharply, often by an order of magnitude, shortly after dark. This mass nocturnal drift may be evidence of an adaptive strategy whereby invertebrates find new feeding sites, or relief from fractious brethren or overcrowded conditions, while protected by darkness from the mouths of predators. Like Huck Finn, they give themselves to the river, traveling by night. Vast quantities of creatures are involved in the drift. An enterprising researcher once bulldozed a hundred and sixty yards of a Swedish river to clear it of all fauna, then measured the repopulation by drift. After eleven days he found up to 7,400 invertebrates per square yard, which for the whole stretch of river extrapolates to a pioneering influx of four million tiny animals with a biomass of about ten pounds.

In broad ecological terms, the drift may simply be a system's way of sloughing off the excess above its carrying capacity. But with a continuous and very substantial removal of organisms down the gutter, how do populations maintain themselves? Why aren't headwaters and upper reaches depleted? It seems that compensating behaviors have evolved. Mayflies, stoneflies, and many other insects characteristically fly upstream to lay their eggs, and some insects migrate upstream in both their aquatic and aerial stages. Trout generally swim upstream to spawn. Nearly all aquatic animals instinctively face into the current, and so to move at all means initially to move upstream. Snails have been observed to travel upriver, maybe as far as one mile in a year. *Gammurus*, a small crustacean, undertakes mass migrations against the current, sticking close to the bank and overcoming riffles with the help of turbulence and eddies.

The dimensions of this counter-drift behavior were once illuminated, almost literally, by an experiment involving radioactive phosphorous. One week after irradiated bacteria were introduced into a Michigan river, radioactive invertebrates were detected a hundred yards upstream. A week later the radiation had advanced to two hundred yards and was showing up in different organisms. It progressed more quickly through quiet waters than it did through a long riffle. In five weeks' time, contaminated stoneflies and fishflies were detected as far as five hundred yards above the point of introduction—an extended biotic exclamation up one of the gutters of entropy, at what cost to the radiated ecosystem no one knows.

Pacific salmon come from a long lineage. The oldest species known by fossil, *Eosalmo driftwoodensis*, lived fifty million years ago, while Oregon was still tectonically assembling itself. The most dramatic family member to date was *Smilodonicthys rastrosus*, a lunker species that has caused many sport fishermen to investigate time travel. This fish, which swam our waters five or six million years ago, was ten feet long, weighed five hundred pounds, and was equipped with long fangs—the saber-toothed tiger of salmonids.

Salmon as we know them probably evolved in the course of the last two million years. By one theory, they derive from freshwater fish that took to sea out of Pleistocene necessity, displaced by glaciers from their native lakes and rivers. Others argue that their anadromous habit is much older, but at some point in evolutionary time, salmonids acquired the capacity to survive in both salt and fresh water and to orient themselves on epic North Pacific travels. It still isn't known how they navigate at sea. Sensitivity to the sun or stars seems unlikely. It may be, some researchers believe, that salmon are somehow attuned to Earth's magnetic field, following pathways of extremely low-voltage current that eventually return them to the mouths of their native river systems. Close to shore and in fresh water they probably proceed by means of sensitivity to temperature changes and direction of flow, but mainly by an exquisite sense of smell capable of discerning the unique chemical signature of their home waters.

The Pleistocene glaciers left a desolate landscape of gravels and bare basalt. As grasses and shrubs and trees gradually dispersed from unglaciated refugia, salmon pioneered the reopened waterways, adapting to the nuances of individual drainages, fertilizing the gravels with spawn and their spawned-out bodies. Willows and other riparian vegetation slowly took hold, stabilizing banks and bars. Millennia passed, salmon thronging the rivers in enormous runs that interblended throughout the year. Eventually conifers stood near streams again, their shade moderating water temperatures as the climate warmed, their toppled trunks restraining the erosive power of floods, trapping gravels, forming pools and riffles. Young salmon came of age in the structured streams, gaining strength for their journey by feeding on the carcasses of the old. Raccoons and bears and eagles came for the carcasses, dispersing the rich captured life of the North Pacific deep into woods and mountains. Old-growth forests and mountain meadows are transmutations of the bones and flesh of countless salmon.

A forest or meadow ecosystem, any ecosystem, is a complex abundance tuned toward its own persistence. The system does not immunize its member species and individuals against disaster, but it does weave its lifeways into a many-stranded resilience capable of absorbing disaster and easing its harshest blows. Fire in a healthy prairie or forest is normally not a catastrophe but an agent of renewal, a destroying creator, and floods in a healthy watershed are the same kind of force. They flush sediment downstream and onto the floodplain, where it fertilizes vegetation. They claim new driftwood and rearrange wood already in the river, forming new pools and deepening existing ones, reinvigorating their food webs. And spring flood surges carry millions of juvenile salmon, called smolt, hundreds of miles to the sea—the smolt, with little strength yet, face upstream, relying solely on the current to get them where they need to go.

The specific means by which floods renew stream ecosystems are still largely unknown. Researchers discover them piecemeal, one at a time, through dedication and good luck. A recent study involved the October caddis, a large orange insect relished by adult steelhead. (The steelhead is a large anadromous form of trout; a trout is a salmon that stayed in the river.) In the spring, caddis larvae graze periphyton like sheep in a pasture. Smaller species of insects get little to eat and fare poorly, and young steelhead, who rely on those small insects (the caddis is too big for them, and too well armored in its case of silk and pebbles) also do poorly. They grow slowly. But if there comes a winter flood of sufficient magnitude to roll sizable rocks in its bedload, those rocks will smash a great many October caddis cases while doing less damage to smaller insects, which find refuge in cracks and depressions. In the spring the smaller insects will get a greater share of periphyton forage, young steelhead will get more to eat and fatten faster, and the steelhead species—along with steelhead fishermen, among other scavengers and predators—will have been well served by the violence of rushing water.

The dams we humans build are intended to restrain that violence, and they mainly succeed, to our benefit. But they also mute or eliminate altogether the ecological benefits of floods, and a hundred and fifty years of accumulating economic activity has dramatically amplified the damage floods do. The draining and conversion of wetlands for agriculture has forfeited the absorptive value of those natural sponges and laid their soil open to erosion. Building roads along rivers and hardening their channels with levees and dikes merely exports the power of floods downstream. In the watersheds of the Cascades and Coast Range, clearcuts and logging roads have increased peak stream flows by twenty to thirty percent. A clearcut slope releases ten times the sediment a forested slope will; the hemorrhage declines over time but does not fully heal for thirty years. Logging roads are even more damaging, boosting the chance of landslides by ten to a hundredfold. Logging road mileage in Oregon national forests has more than tripled since 1960. The total now stands at over 73,000 miles.

Erosion in mountain watersheds is naturally periodic, most of it taking place in concentrated bursts during major deluges. In watersheds riddled with roads and clearcuts, as virtually all of ours are, those epochal storms can cause wildly cascading destruction. Two hours of the benchmark flood of 1964 produced twice as much erosion as would occur in the next thirty *years* combined. The flood of February 1996, though lesser than the 1964 event, will likely tell a similar story when studies are completed, and future floods will repeat the tale. Huge river and stream flows are nothing unusual in Oregon. In the flood of 1861, the Willamette River's discharge at Albany was measured at nearly triple the 1996 peak level. A current ran four feet deep through downtown Salem. Every mill in Oregon City was swept away. In 1907 there were three floods in a single year, two of them bigger than 1996. Since 1860 there have been some fourteen Oregon floods of the 1996 magnitude or greater, an average of one per decade.

Salmon evolved with floods and by means of floods. Like volcanism and the great ice flows, high water has never daunted them for long, but in this eye blink of evolutionary time we call human they face grave troubles. A century of logging has suffocated their spawning gravels with silt and raised the crucial water temperatures of formerly shaded streams. A century and a half of ranching and farming has denuded and broken down stream banks, turning cold deep flows into warm shallows, and laced stream waters with harmful fertilizers. Riverside industries have exposed salmon to chemical effluents that nothing in their evolutionary past has prepared them for. Dams on the Columbia kill nine out of ten smolt on their migratory journey; dams on the Snake, Deschutes, Klamath, and Middle Fork of the Willamette have walled salmon away from major portions of their ancestral habitat. Hatchery fish crowd out the wild populations, spread diseases among them, and dilute their finely tuned genetic heritage through hybridization. Wild salmon still return to their birth waters, but in ragtag remnants of their former runs. The waters no longer support them. The home they made in the Pleistocene is falling apart.

The Little Deschutes River

July 1993

Although this is a protected river, in some places the forest has been heavily cut—right to the river's edge. Much of the river flows through wetlands. Not until my third trip here did I discover this meadow along the river, and I probably couldn't return to it now without a lot of searching. Such a pristine landscape is both eerie and inviting. Wolf lichen adorns the snags.

The North Fork of the Owyhee River
October 1989

The North Fork of the Owyhee is small, the canyon rocky and steep. Cattle can't get in here, so the native bunch grass is still untrammeled and healthy. Tangled wild grapevines tumble toward the river; lichens and desert varnish color the wall.

THE SYCAN RIVER
MAY 1993

This river has a dramatically diverse character. Originating on Winter Ridge, the river floods into Sycan Marsh, a twenty-four-thousand-acre wetland managed by the Nature Conservancy. Farther downstream, the stretch that I hiked flows through a basalt gorge with monumental old-growth ponderosa pines. It's these relatively inaccessible canyons that harbor most of the old growth that remains in Eastern Oregon.

ELKHORN CREEK

FEBRUARY 1997

This rugged canyon is nearly inaccessible. Hiking in the riverbed, following its tunnel through an ancient forest maze, is the most feasible way to go. Mosses, lichens, and ferns are everywhere, in amazing variety. Here one sees what the forests of the lower Cascade Range used to look like. I found a half-mile stretch of river so inspiring I camped there for three days, despite drizzle and snowfall, and made more than 230 exposures.

The Wallowa River
May 1992

The Wallowa flows fast through deep canyons of basalt. Forests of fir, larch, and pine alternate with meadows and hillsides of wildflowers. The river has both state and federal protection. This dual coverage has been a boon for wildlife, and anglers are pleased that populations of steelhead have recovered in recent years. Unfortunately, railroad tracks and telephone poles interrupt the landscape along the entire stretch we paddled, and the rim and upper hills are studded with enormous power transmission towers. These compromises in the wildness of the river bother me, so I eliminated them in this shot. Photographs don't always tell the whole truth.

The White River

April 1990

The White River Glacier on the southwest flank of Mount Hood gives birth to this river. It cascades through a lush forest of hemlock and fir, then through drier terrain with ponderosa pine and white oak, and eventually down to the Oregon High Desert, where the forest thins to juniper and sage. From the vantage of river runners in particular this is a dramatic transition. The entire length is protected except for one spectacular ninety-foot waterfall upstream of this view, where a proposed hydroelectric project has been granted a permit.

The North Fork of the Umpqua River
April 1990

The North Fork of the Umpqua is surrounded by wilderness and roadless areas. In springtime, hundreds of feeder streams tumble into the river, and the woods alongside are full of native dogwoods with creamy white flowers, blooming wild azaleas, and pink rhododendrons.

FISH CREEK

SEPTEMBER 1990

Fish Creek flows intermittently and is generally dry at this time of year. Beaver ponds upstream from this site create permanent water sources for wildlife. The warm cast in this image is from late afternoon light. Many forest fires were burning throughout the West, and the sunsets this particular autumn were very red.

The Little North Fork of the Santiam River
July 1990

Conservationists and the timber industry have fought over this watershed for more than twenty years. Legislative attempts in 1975 and 1979 both failed to protect the Little North Fork of the Santiam as a state scenic waterway; on the third attempt, in 1985, legislation finally passed. Opal Creek, a key upstream tributary, received federal protection in 1996. The Opal Creek and the Bull of the Woods wilderness areas provide a healthy upstream watershed of ancient forest that helps preserve the water quality of this river. The Little North Fork of the Santiam runs clear even during winter storm floods, as few rivers do these days.

The low flows of summer reveal this gorge of polished basalt. The rounded hollow on the right side of the photograph is a whirling eddy at high water, when rocks and gravel swirl around, drilling into the bedrock.

Quartzville Creek

This creek has a uniquely beautiful character because of its many meanders and mossy outcroppings of rock. The geology once attracted gold miners. The protected segment of Quartzville Creek, joined here by a tributary from the left, is classified as "recreational" because of the highway alongside and considerable logging in the corridor.

THE MALHEUR RIVER
JULY 1993

This riverside offers spacious grassy meadows full of wildflowers to stroll through. Old-growth ponderosa pines still stand here. For eight years I hiked and paddled these fifty-six rivers, and I can honestly report that there isn't much ancient forest left. I was continually saddened to find stumps where there should have been an abundance of gigantic old trees. The white blossoms in the river are water buttercups growing in floating mats, the only ones like them I've seen.

The Donner und Blitzen River
July 1995

In 1864, U. S. troops crossing this river during a thunderstorm named it "Thunder and Lightning" in German. The river and its Steens Mountain tributaries feed Malheur Lake, where their waters evaporate. The wild and scenic segment ends where the river enters the Malheur Wildlife Refuge; in the refuge, ironically, much of the river's flow is diverted for irrigation. In this photograph, I like the way the junipers march into the distance, and the contrast of the green riparian zone with the drier slopes.

A BRIEF HISTORY OF EDEN

The streams and rivers pictured in this book are among the least disturbed in the Oregon landscape. To preserve their natural character, they have been protected by law from dams, development, and resource extraction. As you view these photographs, you are looking into the rivered land as it is today, and you are looking back through two hundred years at a kind of Eden, at the landscape close to the way it may have been before Euro-American exploration and settlement. But one original element is missing. You see no people in these river places, but a few hundreds or thousands of years ago you would have. These rivers and watersheds were the ancient homes of Northwest Indians, inhabited for longer than they could remember.

Chinookan and Sahaptian peoples lived from the Dalles west along the Columbia, their lives intensely focused on the river. They speared and netted salmon, plied the waters in fifty-foot dugout canoes, traded with tribes from throughout the greater Northwest near the rich fishing waters of Celilo Falls. Eastward, the Tenino made winter villages in the Deschutes and John Day valleys; the Umatilla and Cayuse ranged over the Columbia Plateau; the Nez Perce trapped salmon and dug roots in the canyons of the Wallowa and the Minam, Joseph Creek and the Grande Ronde. Shoshones and Bannocks took salmon from the Snake River, trout and insects from the streams of the Blue Mountains. Nomadic bands of Northern Paiutes wandered Oregon's hardest country, its southeast quarter, gathering cattails, rice grass, and wild cabbage from moist oases by streams and lakes, holing up in winter rock shelters in the Owyhee canyons. Klamaths and Modocs lived in the milder south-central region, harvesting pods of the yellow water lily on Klamath Lake, fishing and lodging on the Sprague, the Williamson, and the little Lost River that can't decide where it wants to go.

West of the Cascades, the Takelma inhabited the Rogue and Applegate and Illinois drainages; their name means "those who dwell along the river." The Umpqua took their living from the two-forked river of that name, running the waters in maneuverable canoes. The Molalla, recent fugitives from the east, were centered in the McKenzie and Santiam and Clackamas watersheds of the western Cascade slope. The great wetland that was the Willamette Valley was home to the nine bands of the Kalapuya, who gathered the edible bulbs of camas and other staples and regularly burned the prairies to keep them vigorous. (Kalapuya means "long grasses.") And along the coast, several peoples—Tututni, Coos, Siuslaw, Alsea, Tillamook, Clatsop, from south to north— lived on salmon, seals, and other bounty of the tidal rivers, from which many bands took their names: Nehalem, Tillamook, Nestucca, Salmon.

All those native cultures depended on rivers, and everything that lured outsiders to the Oregon Country also had to do with rivers. The first seekers were sea captains looking for the Strait of Anian, the Northwest Passage, the legendary channel of commerce wishfully imagined by European lords and monarchs. They came and sailed away on what coastal Indians called "the river with one bank," leaving diseases, a few shipwrecks, and a scattering of their genes. The first seafarer to enter the Columbia, the American Robert Gray, came in quest of sea otter pelts for the China trade. (The otter then ranged upriver to Celilo Falls.) Lewis and Clark arrived with their Corps of Discovery via the Snake and Columbia, finding the salmon "jumping very thick." Though they failed Thomas Jefferson's charge to find "the direct water communication from sea to sea formed by the bed of the Missouri, and perhaps the Oregon," they did discover, in Lewis's phrase, "the most practicable Route such as Nature has permitted." And they did put Oregon, and some of its Columbia Basin rivers, on the map.

From 1811, when John Jacob Astor's men established a trading post at Astoria, through the 1830s, trappers and traders found their way into almost every river valley in Oregon in search of beaver. The Willamette Valley was trapped out quickly. Alexander McLeod, exploring drainages to the south in 1826, was thwarted only by the Siuslaw, which was too choked with fallen trees to penetrate. He was seeking a rumored great southern river that might be navigable for trade—a diminished version of the indomitable Northwest Passage myth. He found the Rogue and was badly disappointed. Peter Skene Ogden also searched for "the big river," which he called the Clammite; he eventually found the headwaters of the Klamath, but no navigable river. Ogden and others thoroughly explored east of the Cascades too, opening trade routes from the Columbia south to Klamath Lake and up the John Day valley into the Malheur drainage. The most significant track pioneered by the trappers led from the Snake River up the Burnt River and Alder Creek to the Powder and the Grande Ronde Valley, then over the Blues to the Umatilla and the Columbia. This route was incorporated into the Oregon Trail.

Methodist missionaries arrived in the 1830s and looked along rivers for what they desired: tillable soil and heathen souls. At French Prairie and the Falls of the Willamette they found good soil but few souls, the Kalapuya having been rendered virtually extinct by Euro-American diseases. That meant little human resistance to the waves of settlers that pulsed annually into the Willamette Valley during the 1840s. The stiffest natural resistance came, cruelly enough, at the end of the six-month trek, when the weakened immigrants were on the verge of success. Before the Barlow Road opened in 1846, they had to take to the Columbia River at the Dalles on rafts or in makeshift boats. The Columbia was a wild river then. Many families lost everything they owned at the Cascades, a three-mile rapid now drowned by Bonneville Dam. A good many lost their lives.

Those who made it spread southward through the New Eden of the Willamette Valley, running livestock in prairie grasses that reached above the animals' backs, building log homes not near the river but along the valley's forested, foothilled margins. Many settlers had been flooded out in the Mississippi Valley; they weren't about to repeat their mistake. The broad and braided Willamette flowed out of its banks regularly, leaving water standing for months in sloughs and oxbows. Later arrivals, forced to claim in the floodplain, set to work digging drainage ditches and gradually brought the moist earth under the plow. As their livelihoods progressed, other lives declined. One settler wrote at midcentury that the valley had "largely ceased to be the home of the crane, curlew, gray plover, and even the snipe, as well as the beaver, muskrat, and wild duck."

Gold was discovered in the Rogue River country in 1851, drawing a brief flurry of prospectors to tributary junctions throughout the watershed, and then in the 1860s richer pay streaks showed themselves in Baker County and on the John Day. Some operations, placer and hard rock, produced millions of dollars in yellow metal over the course of many decades. Ditches up to a hundred miles long were dug to convey water for hydraulic mining, which ate away the sides of stream valleys, and riverbeds were turned upside down by dredging operations. The streams of northeastern Oregon were lucky that their gold was not more plentiful. To see why, visit the Powder River and its tributary, Cracker Creek, near the town of Sumpter. You'll find their channels heaped high with dumps of gravel, cobbles, and boulders, continuous mounds of barren debris that look for all the world like castings from a giant earthworm.

Another kind of mining boom exploded on the Columbia and coastal rivers in the 1860s. Canning technology arrived from California, and with it came industrial salmon fishing. The rivers were rigged and plied with gill nets, pound nets, horse-drawn purse seines, and, on the Columbia, perpetual-motion fish wheels, turned by the current, each capable of scooping out fifty flopping tons of salmon in a single season. The young state's export of canned salmon soared to nearly half a million cases a year by 1878, almost twenty-four million pounds of fish. The runs remained unimaginably huge compared to today, but nonetheless in 1875 the modern era of fishery management was born. The Oregon legislature asked the United States Fish Commission to investigate the diminishing Columbia River salmon runs. The commission recommended a hatchery.

Steamships came to the Columbia, Willamette, and larger coastal rivers in the 1850s, and the U. S. Army Corps of Engineers was recruited to dredge channels and remove many thousands of snags and drift trees. By the 1860s people and freight could travel by steamer up the Willamette to Corvallis (to Eugene at high water), and, with mule or rail portages at the Cascades and Celilo Falls, up the

Columbia and the lower Snake clear to Lewiston, Idaho.

River transport and the railroads that followed encouraged a bounce-back migration into Eastern Oregon, the Willamette Valley being claimed out. Slow at first, the influx quickened once the disagreeable Modocs, Nez Perce, Bannocks, and Shoshones had been subdued in the 1870s. Hopeful ranchers settled by every stream and spring; in twenty years their sheep and cattle had grazed out much of the bunch grass, laying the ecosystem open to the sagebrush and cheat grass that dominate it today. Public lands grazing continued unregulated until 1934 and continues under-regulated now, doing severe injury to rangelands and streams. Dry country takes a long time to heal. Irrigation for pasture and crop farming became a traditional way of life east of the mountains, buttressed by first-in-time water rights. Diversion dams and pumps deplete some rivers and streams to a midsummer trickle. Groundwater is also tapped, lowering the water table and sending runoff loaded with silt, pesticides, and fertilizers into the rivers.

Oregon's timber industry started slowly toward the end of the 1800s. Big riverside old growth was first to fall, Sitka spruce and red cedar and Douglas fir, the mammoth logs rafted downstream to the mills. As cutting proceeded up the lower Coast Range and Cascade slopes, splash dams came into use: a small stream was dammed into a big pond where logs were dumped; the dam was breached and a torrent of logs shot down to the river, leaving a reamed-out channel of mud and bedrock. World War I brought the first big boom, driving up the price of timberland by a factor of ten. Big corpora-

tions bought major holdings and logged them off with little reforestation, punching roads and muddying streams in many watersheds. More than half of Oregon's jobs were wood products jobs. The housing boom after World War II gave the industry another boost and spread clearcuts into previously roadless areas of the national forests, the private holdings having been thoroughly mined. Steeper slopes were sheared, shallower soils exposed, and road after road carelessly built, the bladed earth dumped down the mountainsides. Timber was Oregon's king for a hundred years. The economy prospered, for the most part, but streams will be paying the price of prosperity for decades to come.

And they are paying in other ways. Our century has dammed the Oregon-border portion of the Columbia in four places, turning that stretch of America's third-greatest river into a string of slackwater lakes. Our electrical power is cheap; salmon smolt are riding in barges. Pulp mills and food processing plants contribute jobs and essential products; their effluents contribute poisonous chemicals and smothering nutrient loads. Roads and highways take us anywhere we want to go; roads follow rivers and dike them off from their floodplains, forcing them to incise their channels. In the cities our toilets flush cleanly; during storm flows they flush into rivers. New malls, new roads, new suburban expansion make a good life available for many; they make the land unavailable to absorb water as it did, and now five- to ten-year floods are becoming annual events.

If everything we have done to our rivers in the course of two hundred years had occurred overnight, we would be horrified, grief stricken. But the changes have come gradually, incrementally, hardly perceptible from year to year, from decade to decade. As the changes occur, we adjust. We take as normal the rivers as they now flow through our lives, hardly aware that the river any child grows up with is likely to be muddier, more engineered, more polluted, and less rich in life than the river her father or grandmother knew. The rivers we tax the hardest for our needs and conveniences have been slowly slipping away for a long time, and as they have slipped we have lost our sense of what a healthy river might look like. And so the rivers in this book, the rivers our history has touched least, the wild rivers we have taken measures to legally safeguard from ourselves, are not merely images of beauty. They are surviving standards of our landscape's natural integrity, benchmarks that could guide us as we plan its future.

The Middle Fork of the John Day River
October 1989

The Nature Conservancy commissioned me to photograph ranch land along the Middle Fork of the John Day that it wanted to turn into a preserve. When I arrived, the atmosphere in the valley was thick with dust from log trucks continually hauling out old-growth ponderosa pine on dirt roads. The ranch land, especially along the river-bank, looked like a feedlot, trampled for years by cattle. It would not be easy to make beautiful photographs here. Searching upstream I found this lush riparian area, which the Forest Service had fenced with barbed wire to keep cows out. The Conservancy has since restored the ranch area, which is now flourishing.

THE KLAMATH RIVER
APRIL 1991

I wanted to get to Hells Corner of the Klamath River in springtime, before the canyon was burnt by the sun. Hells Corner, right? Sure to be warm. But I was fooled into going too early. Hells Corner is near the California border, at an elevation of about four thousand feet. I camped in the cold and wet for a few days. Brief bursts of sun came and went between storms. In this photo, sleet makes a soft backdrop for the emerging buds of an Oregon white oak.

THE JOHN DAY RIVER
MAY 1992

This immense basalt canyon offers more than 150 miles of solitude and exploration. Canoeing it, a thousand feet below the rim of the Oregon High Desert, can take two weeks. The lower half of the mainstem John Day is protected by both state and federal law, the longest continuous stretch of protection for any one river in Oregon. More than twenty potential dam sites have been identified on the John Day system. It's no coincidence that the healthiest wild fish system in the Columbia Basin remains undammed.

This photograph was made minutes after a thunderstorm swept past. After unpacking the canoe, I had climbed a hill near the rim in shorts and tee shirt, thinking that I wouldn't be out long. While I was looking for compositions, a lightning storm approached, and I decided I would be safer below. On the way down I abandoned my tripod and cameras, which can act as lightning rods. As soon as the storm passed, I ran for my equipment and made a series of photographs with various lenses as quickly as I could. This forty-five-minute drama was the only worthwhile light in three days of dull overcast weather.

WALKER CREEK
APRIL 1991

Extremely rare in the Oregon Coast Range, wetlands such as Walker Creek are among the most productive ecosystems on Earth. This marsh hosts rare plant species, including Nelson's checker-mallow; the yellow plants visible here are new skunk cabbage. Protection in 1988 as a state scenic waterway prohibited construction of the Walker Creek Dam, a totally unnecessary impoundment that would have flooded this critical habitat. Sadly, though, nearly all the surrounding forest has been recently clearcut, severely endangering the wetland.

THE SANDY RIVER
FEBRUARY 1997

Winter is the best season to find solitude on the Sandy, only fifteen minutes from Portland. Stepping into an old-growth grove, one enters another world. This remnant of low-elevation ancient forest is preserved by the Nature Conservancy. I made the photograph during a brief lull in the rain. The river is just beyond these trees: its open space provides the backlighting.

EAGLE CREEK

OCTOBER 1993

This photograph was made on a sunny and still autumn morning in the high alpine zone of the Wallowa Mountains; the bright granite slabs bounced light into the shadows, adding warmth to the scene. The plant with the red foliage is alpine fleece flower, found throughout the higher elevations of northeastern Oregon. Both limber pine and whitebark pine eke out an existence here. At the head of Eagle Creek, where it flows out of Eagle Lake, hikers find a very unwild and unscenic dam.

The North Fork of the Malheur River
June 1992

The upper North Fork of the Malheur has parklike stands of ponderosa pine with meadows of flowering spike rush and false hellebore. The uppermost stretch is rich with wetlands. This is one of the extremely rare places where I found large-diameter ponderosa pine and western larch. Still remote and wild, the area through which the North Fork flows is worthy of its proposed wilderness status.

THE GRANDE RONDE RIVER
MAY 1991

The lovely Grande Ronde begins in the Elkhorn Range of the Blue Mountains. The moist ecosystem of the upper stretch is heavily forested. The forest then thins, giving way to grassy hillsides, and disappears as you drop in elevation and move east into the rain shadow of the Blues. I saw more wildlife here than in any other area that I photographed for this book: black bear, elk, river otters, ospreys, falcons, hawks, and eagles. The Grande Ronde figures prominently in efforts to aid the recovery of Snake River salmon and steelhead.

Along with the usual minor excitements of running rivers, I had one tense moment on this four-day canoe trip—high-centering on rocks in the middle of a rapid. Rescuing a fully loaded and swamped canoe can be like wrestling a freight train to shore. My companion, who had never experienced white water before, had to jump out of the canoe, swim the rest of the rapid to the bank, and then hike back upstream to a point opposite me. I tossed him the throw rope, which he wrapped around a tree, and we swung the canoe like a pendulum to shore.

The North Fork of the Powder River
October 1991

Late in October, I drove up a steep, rough road to backpack into the Elkhorn Range of the Blue Mountains. The North Powder originates there, and I thought I could make photographs looking down-canyon, where the western larches—deciduous conifers—would be ablaze with bright, rusty-yellow needles.

The light rain had turned to snow by the time I reached the summit ridge at dusk. Setting up my three-season bivy tent, I slithered in for a long cold night of sleeplessness. The wind howled, the tent flapped, snowy spindrift came through the mosquito netting and settled on my sleeping bag. Getting up at the first hint of dawn, I made my usual quart of coffee and powdered cocoa and stood in frozen boots, eight inches deep in a near blizzard. I had a bad feeling about the condition of the road out, but I wanted pictures. The storm abated in a few hours, and I began photographing. I hiked most of the day just below the mountainous ridges of the aptly named North Powder. This, my favorite photograph from the trip, shows the frozen image of what the canyon must look like four to six months of the year.

The Wenaha River

September 1993

This tributary to the Grande Ronde flows through a canyon sixteen hundred feet deep in the Wenaha-Tucannon Wilderness. Snowberry, the red bush on the hillside, is an important browse for the bighorn sheep, deer, and elk that winter here. The Wenaha is a critical spawning ground for the salmon and steelhead of the Grande Ronde watershed.

THE NORTH FORK OF THE CROOKED RIVER
AUGUST 1991

The North Fork of the Crooked flows for thirteen miles through a wilderness study area, and its remote canyon is seldom visited. Camping here for several days in hot, clear summer weather, I began to lose patience with the conditions and the terrain. Because the canyon is so deep, the sun doesn't reach the river until midmorning, and by that time of day in early August the light was too bright to make good photographs. On the fourth morning I awoke at 4:30 to find clouds obscuring the stars, which promised soft light, low in contrast, perfect for photographing in the woods.

Hiking up and over a ridge, I could see this clump of trees and grass below. It looked promising, but the cloudy sky was suddenly turning bright. I ran down the hillside and set up the tripod and camera quickly, making six exposures from two different perspectives. At home, I found two exposures were a little dark, two were somewhat overexposed, and two were unacceptably contrasty because of direct sunlight. I chose one of the dark transparencies and lightened it up in the darkroom, filtering out an excessive blue cast.

A Place in the Rivered Land

The protection of rivers was a late-blooming priority in the history of the twentieth-century conservation movement, despite the fact that several of its formative battles were sparked by dam-building projects. In 1913 the damming of the Tuolumne River in the California Sierra Nevada, and the consequent inundation of Yosemite's Hetch Hetchy Valley, aroused cries of outrage from John Muir and his young Sierra Club. Forty years later, a proposal for two dams in Dinosaur National Monument forged conservationists into a broad activist coalition and brought the modern movement of age. The issue in each case, though, was less the river itself than the sanctity of the national park through which it flowed. Conservationists were focused on setting aside entire parcels of land as parks and wilderness, and most of those parcels were in high-elevation mountainous terrain with streams but few long stretches of river. Rivers flowed through the hard-worked valleys where we lived; parks and wilderness were somewhere else, where we went to get away.

By midcentury, though, American rivers had been so thoroughly dredged, channelized, filled, polluted, dammed, and diverted that a movement arose to protect the freest and purest stretches that remained. The original intent, modeled on the idea of wilderness designation, was to set aside the crown jewels—the singular, spectacularly wild rivers of our part of the continent. That idea was expanded in the 1960s to include reaches of river that had seen some development but were still free flowing and hadn't lost their wild character. The Wild and Scenic Rivers Act passed Congress in 1968 with the enthusiastic assent of President Lyndon Johnson, designating sections of twelve rivers as charter members of the National Wild and Scenic Rivers System and identifying others for study. The act recognized three classes of protected status: wild rivers, defined as "vestiges of primitive America;" scenic rivers, less wild but largely undeveloped; and recreational rivers, readily accessible and generally more developed. Among the original twelve was an eighty-four mile section of the lower Rogue, preserving its dramatic passage through the Klamath Mountains to the Pacific.

The Wild and Scenic Rivers Act shields designated rivers from dams, hydroelectric diversions, channelization, and other harmful impacts on the river itself. As for land uses along the river, the managing public agencies—as many as fifteen may be involved in a single river—generally grandfather in existing uses but limit or prohibit new or expanded uses. A protective corridor extends one-quarter mile to each side of the river, or rim to rim of the river's canyon if it has one. On federal lands, no logging can occur within the corridor of a wild river; scenic and recreational classifications permit limited logging. Restrictions on mining are similar; claims existing prior to designation are not extinguished. Recreational access may be limited at an agency's discretion to prevent overuse of the river and its corridor. Private water rights are unaffected, except that the government secures to itself the right to maintain instream flow.

From the original twelve in 1968, the Wild and Scenic Rivers System has grown to include some 330 stretches of rivers and tributaries. Oregon's share of these is out of proportion to its size: fifty-six designated rivers and tributaries. (Counts vary among agencies and conservationists because the components of a watershed can be broken down, on a map, in different ways.)

The Oregon system grew slowly at first. In 1975, with the creation of Hells Canyon National Recreation Area, the Hells Canyon portion of the Snake joined the Rogue as our second listed river (and thereby escaped a dam already authorized for the lower canyon). Reaches of the Illinois and Owyhee

were designated as part of wilderness legislation in 1984. And then the deluge. Jimmy Carter, late in his presidency, had called for an expanded wild and scenic system, spurring the Forest Service and other federal agencies to evaluate thousands of rivers for possible inclusion. The Oregon Rivers Council (now the Pacific Rivers Council) used Forest Service studies to persuade Senator Mark Hatfield to sponsor the Oregon Omnibus Rivers Act of 1988, which in one fell swoop added stretches of forty-four rivers plus nine tributaries to the national system, the most ever brought under protection at one time outside of Alaska.

That same year, conservationist Bill Marlett and the Oregon Natural Resources Council launched a successful ballot initiative that expanded the Oregon Scenic Waterways System, which provides overlapping safeguards at the state level for several federally listed rivers, and constitutes the only protection for a handful of others, including the Nestucca on the north coast. It was an altogether phenomenal year for the flowing waters of our state, an environmental achievement that deserves to rank alongside the landmark bottle bill and land use planning legislation of the 1970s. Oregon's breakthrough placed it in the forefront of river conservation nationally and inspired similar omnibus efforts in several other states.

And yet, nearly a decade after that breakthrough, the Oregon wild and scenic system is nothing very vast. Of thirty-five thousand miles of streams and rivers big enough to bear names, only 1,850 miles, or five percent, are included in the system. That far exceeds the national figure of six-tenths of one percent, but it's a large number only by comparison.

Why, after the most successful river conservation campaign in history, and the heightened public awareness that came with it, do ninety-five percent of our river miles remain unprotected?

The answers have to do with natural resources and land ownership. On federal lands, where most of our eligible rivers flow, wild and scenic designation raises a limited but real impediment to logging, mining, and grazing. Resource industries historically have had easy access to raw materials on public lands, due to a tilted doctrine of multiple use. That tilt has begun to correct itself, but institutional inertia and industry lobbying still exert a powerful drag against change. The Forest Service has identified a hundred Oregon river sections, beyond those already designated, eligible for wild and scenic consideration. Only three have been designated since 1988. The process grinds slowly through year after year of studies, hearings, and stalemate.

Private land ownership is another sticking point. The Wild and Scenic Rivers Act was intended to put a cap on development, not to eliminate development already in place, and the government's favored tool toward that end is the purchase of easements that disallow new or intensified construction on private holdings along designated rivers. But the act also authorizes outright land aquisition through eminent domain. That power has been used sparingly, mostly in the first few years of the act's existence, and usually to block large-scale development presenting a major threat to a river's natural character. But the knowledge that eminent domain can be and has been asserted makes property owners understandably skittish about the prospect of wild and scenic designation. They might be more receptive if the government were to renounce eminent domain and work with easements only, emphasizing to land owners that a river whose natural integrity has been secured for the future against unwanted encroachments of commerce will enhance, not diminish, the value of their holdings.

———————

But Oregon's wild and scenic system will continue to grow, if slowly. Far more troubling than the limited extent of the system is its limited effectiveness as a shield against ecological injury. Wild and scenic status has blocked dams and other engineering projects on several Oregon rivers, but it has been much less successful in preventing less dramatic, more gradual degradation. Logging and overgrazing occur, illegally and legally, within the designated half-mile corridors of some of our listed rivers, and they occur close outside the corridors of almost all of them. A quarter-mile is the distance you can walk, at a brisk pace, in five minutes. You can drive it in fifteen seconds. Clearcutting, road building, mining, and intensive grazing that close to a river directly affect the river itself. Human beings may or may not respect a line on a map. Sediment, debris torrents, mine contamination, and sun-heated water definitely do not.

And that is only the lateral dimension. A river is a creature of length, a continuity, but only a scant few of our listed streams are designated from source to mouth, and most of those are short tributaries. Most of the rivers are protected only in a section or two, usually along their upper reaches on public lands; their middle and lower reaches, where we tend to live, receive the accumulating uses and abuses of our economic activity. It is a very good thing that forty miles of the upper Rogue River have been protected since 1988. It is a great thing that eighty-four miles of the lower Rogue have been protected since 1968. But only a third of those miles are managed as wild river, the rest enjoying only weaker protection, and the undesignated remainder of the river, its ninety-mile midsection, is not protected at all. The Rogue's water quality was declining before its listing and has continued to decline since. Its salmon and steelhead runs, with sporadic annual exceptions, have dropped more sharply since designation than they had been dropping before. The Rogue is still a great river, one of the most beautiful rivers in the world, but no ecologist would call it a healthy river.

Health is a relative condition, of course. The Rogue is a healthier river than many. Its listing as wild and scenic has almost certainly slowed its ecological decline, and that is a meaningful accomplishment. It should be sobering, though, that the most sanguine judgment that can be made about a thirty-year charter member of the National Wild and Scenic Rivers System is that it may be deteriorating at a reduced pace.

It is at least plausible to draw a line excluding development from an intact patch of land, call it a park or wilderness area, and expect it to retain its ecological health. But rivers will not hold still for sectioning. We engage them at particular places—bends, holes, falls, canyons. The nouns get vaguer when we try to identify longer parts—reaches, stretches—and become geometrically abstract when we divide a river according to political and economic concerns: sections, segments. What is a segment of a river? To isolate a segment on a map and declare it safe is something like declaring your shoulder or upper thigh safe—important, certainly, but nothing to inspire general confidence. To address the health of rivers we must address them in their wholeness—and that means we must deal with ourselves.

Stream ecologists are working out an idea they call the river continuum concept, which suggests that all rivers, or many at least, share a common ecological gradient along their lengths. From the rills and streamlets of origin to the broad river near its mouth, there is evidence that predictable changes in life communities occur. Shaded headwater regions, structured by stones and fallen wood, host a guild of invertebrates known as shredders, who begin to break down the crucial leaf- and needle-fall that fuels the stream's organic economy. Small particles of that matter are filtered from the current far downstream, in the river's middle reaches, by a guild of collectors. The wider channel receives more sunlight in these reaches, producing more organic matter from within. Periphyton grows more abundantly, supporting a guild of grazers, and various plants take root in sediments the milder-sloped river now deposits. Lower still, where the accomplished river travels its floodplain, its ecology grades into further changes only poorly understood, that zone of the continuum having been less studied and usually more disturbed by human activity.

The science of stream ecology is less than fifty years old, and the river continuum concept is one of its newest hypotheses. It needs testing, refinement, elaboration, but its essential premise seems valid:

rivers have something like a common genotype, a graded biological form associated with their graded fluvial form from source to mouth. The lives and systems of lives you find at a particular place are not arbitrary; they are flourishing where they belong in the organism that is the river.

And where do we humans belong? How do we belong, and how should we belong? It is not arbitrary that we live as closely associated with rivers as we do. As far back as ancient Egypt and Babylonia, and no doubt farther, our civilizations have been built on the floodplains of rivers, on the ruins of continents slowly on their way to the sea. In the modern world our relationship with rivers extends from the high dendritic branchings of their drainages down along each valley and meander to the rich mixed waters of their estuaries. For better or worse, we are members of the river continuum. So far it has been better for us, worse for the rivers and their other members. For that there is plenty of blame to go around. All of us have taken rivers for granted. All of us have participated in their exploitation. The light I'm writing by, the paper I'm writing on, the studs and rafters in the house around me—these and much more have come to me at some cost to rivers, rivers I regularly notice and admire without thinking how my way of life might burden them.

But none of us, not one of us, ever set out deliberately to harm a river. We only set out to live our lives, and, despite all we have done to them, we love the rivers of our home state. We are never far from the lilt and swirl of living water. Whether to fish or swim or paddle, or only to stand and gaze, to glance as we cross a bridge, all of us are drawn to rivers, all of us happily submit to their spell. We need their familiar mystery. We need their fluent lives interflowing with our own.

The National Wild and Scenic Rivers System is an expression of our love, a first, halting recognition of our own excesses and the vulnerability of rivers. In those unwieldy categories of law—wild, scenic, recreational—we are groping toward a right relationship, one that acknowledges our legitimate uses but sets careful limits on them. We are groping toward responsible membership, and we must find our way further. We are gradually learning to cherish wild rivers, such as those you see in this book. Those fountains of natural happiness must always run free. But we fail those rivers if we continue to fail their lower reaches, the valleys where we work and live, the rivers of home. The river above and the river below are the same river. The river is always one, and we fail it if we fail to rejoin its segments, to expand its corridor, to follow the fingering of water into land and learn its way of belonging, that the continuum might flow on with us as part of it. Rivers contain no answers, but if we learn from them the right questions, the answers will flow from ourselves.

The Imnaha River
May 1990

This sensuous landscape runs from the river's headwaters among the highest peaks of the Wallowa Mountains down to the bottom of Hells Canyon, where the Imnaha meets the Snake River. The entire segment, including the south fork, is protected, unusual for such a long river.

Spring is my favorite time here, because the hillsides are fresh with young grass. The weather is changeable and dramatic, as it was on the day I made this photograph. The sun shone bright between storms of black clouds, classic silver linings, and lightning and thunder.

The McKenzie River
September 1990

This image was made at dusk, with so little light it required a thirty-second exposure. The fog in the background formed as the temperature dropped at twilight; a few minutes earlier there had been none.

Well upstream of this site, a large hydroelectric project diverts the river into a tube. An official sign alleges that the river mysteriously disappears at that point, flowing underground and resurfacing downstream. The river does disappear, and does resurface downstream in a magnificent aquamarine pool, but to call the disappearance a "mystery" is doublespeak. Without the diversion, the river would probably always have water in its channel.

THE NORTH FORK OF THE JOHN DAY RIVER
JUNE 1989

I took this photograph on my first white-water trip with my wife, Colleen. I had bought a used Bluehole canoe from a friend so that she could accompany me on some photographic expeditions. Having paddled many difficult Class IV and V rivers in a kayak, I figured a Class II-plus would be easy enough. The river was very bony and shallow, though, and on the first day we broached in a rapid. A fully loaded two-person canoe does not handle like a kayak, and coordinating movements with another paddler was trickier than I had expected. My head knew what to do but my mouth wouldn't speak. Wham—we were high-centered on a boulder.

Days later, hiking the dry canyon hillsides, we found lots of little gardenlike areas full of yellow monkeyflowers and mock orange. The bright overcast made this photograph work by lowering contrast.

The Minam River

I've always loved looking down upon clouds from high ridges. The clouds swirl around and are swept up the slopes or drawn into canyons, where they hunker down and slowly disappear. In sunlight, they are magical. In this first snowstorm of the year, ten inches fell overnight, and cold air trapped in the canyon created these clouds. Because the contrast range of Fujichrome slide film is so narrow, I exposed for the highlights, leaving very dark shadow areas.

The Powder River
October 1991

From far above the river, the entrance to a remote canyon can be seen, an important wintering area for waterfowl, deer, and antelope. A native population of rainbow trout survives here. This eleven-mile length of canyon is the only protected segment and the only undeveloped habitat left along 130 miles of river. Upstream, the river is in incredibly poor condition due to gold dredging in the nineteenth century. The piles of rubble left behind are so polluted that ecologists feel the safest course is to leave them undisturbed, for fear of releasing toxic substances into the river.

CRESCENT CREEK

MAY 1993

In May the skies here are stormy and full of gorgeous clouds, the light soft but dramatic. The river bottom is very uneven, criss-crossed with sunken logs and pocketed with invisible deep holes. At the end of a second long day in the water, I finally found the jewel I was looking for, although finding a place to set up a tripod wasn't easy: vantage points were limited to these tiny marshy islands.

THE LITTLE BLITZEN RIVER
JULY 1995

This two-thousand-foot gorge on Steens Mountain was carved by Ice Age glaciers, not by the little creek that exists today. Birds of prey and curl-leaf mountain mahogany perch on these cliffs, which seem to be painted by bright-colored lichens and guano. The extensive blue shadows result from the cliffs being illuminated by the blue sky rather than direct sunlight.

The North Fork of the Middle Fork of the Willamette River
October 1990

I made two trips to this river, which flows out of the Waldo Lake Wilderness. The first was during a rainy week in October, when I made several excellent photographs just around the corner from this view. The river was running high, and the bigleaf maples were at their peak color. The river was muddy, though, from intensive logging upstream, so a week later I revisited the site. The water had dropped and was running clear, but I was disappointed to find the maples had lost most of their leaves. Downstream, however, I found these few trees in a protected hollow. It was drizzling and quite dark when I made this ten-second exposure.

The South Fork of the John Day River
July 1992

After three trips, I still wasn't satisfied with any of my photographs of this river, so I went back to my archives to see if there was something I'd missed. I had often considered printing this transparency, but felt that it was a little "soft" because of the breeze. Once I printed it, I grew to love its romantic, painterly feeling, which is due to the mottled light on the vegetation. The scent given off by these flowering mock orange shrubs is exquisite.

The South Fork of the McKenzie River
October 1990

These sedges have always attracted me. The little tufted islands of color repeating themselves are very appealing. Their delicate blades are usually waving with the river breezes and thus are difficult to photograph. Waiting for them to hold still can test your patience. This overcast day was accommodatingly windless.

The Snake River
May 1991

The Snake ranks among the best river trips in North America; its spectacular gorge is one of the deepest on Earth. An enormous volume of water flushes through the canyon in the spring. Paddling or floating the river requires a permit, for which you must compete with many other private and commercial parties. Ironically, jet boats can roar up and down long sections of the river without need of a permit.

I have kayaked the Snake many times and have more photographs of it than of any other river. For twenty years, I have looked for compositions like this—grassy ridges in soft, sunny light, no wind stirring the vegetation, and in the distance, a river winding out of sight. When I find one, it's one of the purest pleasures I know.

THE SPIRIT OF RIVERS

Anything in nature reflects the viewer, but of all the natural forms, rivers give back the fullest reflection of the human. They are lives in motion, bound up like ours in time and consequence, steadily being born and steadily dying. They stir in their sleep, they laugh and mourn, and—like us at our best—they are true to themselves under all conditions, changeful and changeless, free and constrained, a resurgent presence of past and future made one. To seek a river's source is to seek our own, to turn and turn and always return—to snow and mountains, to sea and sky, and always to water, always to the soul's deep springs, always to the flowing ungraspable image that forever runs free of all names and knowing, singing the story of its own being, bearing forth from distant passages its mortal and infinite nature.

PHOTOGRAPHER'S NOTES

In 1963 the Sierra Club published *The Place No One Knew*, edited and designed by David R. Brower. This book of Eliot Porter's photographs of Glen Canyon on the Colorado River indicted our society for foolishly damming and flooding one of the most beautiful places on earth. Porter's images were my first revelation in color landscape photography; looking at them, I wanted my camera, like his, to make a plea for wild areas.

When Porter called his images "intimate landscapes," I thought he was referring to their emphasis on foreground (sometimes to the exclusion of any background at all). In working on this book, I have come to see additional meanings for the phrase, including deep knowledge and love. An artist who knows and loves his or her subject can perhaps come closer to doing it justice.

In 1988, motivated by Oregon's landmark river legislation, I began making photographs for a book to celebrate our rivers. This project has provided me the opportunity for a long-term immersion in intimate landscapes. I have made repeated visits to all of the fifty-six designated wild and scenic rivers in Oregon, hiking along (and often in) the rivers, roaming up and down the canyons and drainages surrounding them, seeking to capture on film the contours and facets of landscape that make up a river system. I also kayaked and canoed many of the rivers in order to visit remote sections.

For me, a good river trip lasts two or three times as long as others recommend. For example, most people float a thirty-five-mile stretch of the Rogue River in three days. I spent eight days floating it. Reserving the morning and evening for photography, I usually paddled only during midday. Hikes up above river camps added varying perspectives to complement the views from below. I filled a lot of days this way.

A typical summer day in the field starts in the dark at 4:30 AM, regardless of weather. Many photographs can be made before sunrise. I carry all my gear in a backpack and a front waist pack. Lenses, film, and polarizers are up front, because I need them every few minutes. I generally roam all around the area I'm camping in, particularly in the river itself, shooting as long as the light has the quality I'm after. That may last only two or three hours on a clear, sunny day, or all day if there are clouds or fog to filter the sunlight. At midday I nap for one to three hours while waiting for the light to soften again. Then I shoot until dark, eat dinner as quickly as I can, and bed down immediately so as to sleep as long as I can before the next dawn.

My favorite light to work with is bright yet low in contrast. This light occurs with fog, particularly as it burns off. Another variation occurs during the brief interval between overcast and sunlight, and the occasional thin spots in a storm system. More than half the photographs in this book were made beneath overcast skies. (Searching for such light is one reason I may take from three to six days to make a photograph I'm satisfied with.) I will also work right through a rain- or snowstorm—the precipitation softens and filters light—clamping a large umbrella over my tripod to protect my camera. A fourth lighting condition, the perennial favorite of many photographers, is first and last light, when the angle of the sun near the horizon mutes the contrast that midday heightens.

My travels held many surprises. At most rivers, there were very few people, often no one at all. At some, there were intolerable crowds. I found riversides where I felt as though I was the first to witness that paradise, and others so littered or abused I couldn't wait to leave. And although I was alone and walking quietly, I rarely saw wildlife.

I also experienced endless days of awe and astonishment. I was amazed at the rich diversity of ecosystems. The obvious and prevalent degradations notwithstanding, communion with these rivers always restored my spirit. I found great beauty at all of them. Oregon has saved an exceptional number of rivers, a model of stewardship which could be emulated by other states. I feel I could not live without these rivers. It breaks my heart to see them abused, and I rejoice when they are whole.

Every photograph in this book was made within the corridor of one of Oregon's designated wild and scenic river segments. Though these segments are among the least disturbed landscapes in the state, they are not entirely pristine. Most of the ancient forest is gone; only remnants are left. Some of the river channels have been scoured down to bedrock by log drives. Cattle grazing has eradicated much of the native vegetation that was once found along the riparian zones. The bunch grass is largely gone and sagebrush now dominates. I was dismayed to see

livestock in over half of the rivers. Finally, upstream dams and diversions have no doubt shaped the rivers in ways my camera does not reveal. It is likely that no more than twenty of these photographs show what the rivers originally looked like.

In exploring the rivers, I used maps from the U.S. Forest Service and the Bureau of Land Management, which have jurisdiction over most of them. Three books were also helpful: William Sullivan's *Exploring Oregon's Wild Areas* (the Mountaineers, 1988); Wendell Wood's *A Walking Guide to Oregon's Ancient Forests* (the Oregon Natural Resources Council, 1991); and *Soggy Sneakers: A Guide to Oregon Rivers*, compiled by the Willamette Kayak and Canoe Club (the Mountaineers, 1994).

All but two of these photographs were made with a medium-format (six centimeters by seven centimeters) Pentax mounted on a large Gitzo tripod. I use Fuji transparency film for its unsurpassed sharpness and color saturation, even though its exposure latitude is extremely narrow. Often an exposure will be both over- and underexposed at the same time; therefore, I must use the film only in low contrast light or be content with solid black shadows. Exposures range from one-sixtieth of a second to thirty seconds, the average being about one second. Setting up a composition that I like usually takes twenty to thirty minutes, sometimes a few hours, and on rare occasions only thirty seconds. I carry three lenses: a wide angle, a normal, and a small telephoto. I also occasionally use a 1.4x teleconverter.

I sometimes use a warming filter to correct the color balance of cool light in shade or heavy overcast, or to compensate for an increase in ultraviolet light when long distances are involved. More often, I use a polarizing filter to control reflections, to increase color saturation, and to manipulate the contrast range.

Ansel Adams likened the negative to a musical score, and the print to a performance. In other words, photographs are made, not taken. Because the final performance or interpretation of the image is highly personal, I do all my own darkroom work. My procedures are elaborate and meticulous: color-balancing, dodging, and burning fine-tune an image.

Masking is one of the most important tools in transparency printing. It involves making a contact black-and-white negative from the original color transparency. I pin-register the new negative to the color original, and then print from this "sandwich" onto Fujichrome paper. The resulting color print has greater highlight and shadow detail. A further benefit is increased edge contrast, which makes the images appear sharper. Sometimes my photographic prints are better than the original transparencies; in these cases, the color separations for this book were made from the prints.

While creating the images for this book, I made eighteen thousand exposures on film. I drove thirty-two thousand miles of road to visit rivers a total of 130 times. The book that began as a labor of love veered toward obsession because I was determined to pay tribute to every single wild and scenic river in the state.

By the middle of 1996, after eight years of photographing rivers, I thought I had them all; then late in the year Elkhorn Creek was added to the federal system, and out I went again.

So here they are: all of the designated wild and scenic rivers of Oregon as of the spring of 1997. It is my greatest wish that many more rivers become protected, rendering this volume incomplete.

ACKNOWLEDGMENTS

Of the many friends of Oregon rivers who helped me with this text, I'm particularly indebted to stream ecologist Stan Gregory, of Oregon State University, and geomorphologist Gordon Grant, of the Pacific Northwest Research Station, U. S. Forest Service, in Corvallis. Both were very generous to a river novice.

David Bayles, Suzanne Fouty, Larry Cooper, Bradley Boyden, Geoff Pampush, and Doug Markle provided key information. Dennis Nelson, Ellen Bishop, Mitch Wolgamott, Frank Boyden, Roger Hamilton, Ron Pribble, and Marilyn Daniel all read parts of the work, caught errors, and made helpful comments. Suzanne Venino was a quick and careful editor.

"Beginnings" draws on *Rivers, Man, and Myths*, by Robert Brittain (Doubleday, 1958); Mircea Eliade's *Patterns in Comparative Religion* (World, 1958); and *The Encyclopedia of Religion*, edited by Eliade (Macmillan, 1987).

"Water Ways" owes most to *Geology of Oregon*, by Elizabeth L. Orr, William N. Orr, and Ewart M. Baldwin (Kendall Hunt, 1992); *Streams: Their Dynamics and Morphology*, by Marie Morisawa (McGraw Hill, 1968); and *Water*, by Luna B. Leopold and Kenneth S. Davis (Time-Life, 1980). Also helpful was *The Great Floods: Cataclysms of the Ice Age*, a video produced by Washington State University in cooperation with the National Park Service.

My principal sources for "Life Among the Ruins" were J. David Allan's *Stream Ecology: Structure and Function of Running Waters* (Chapman and Hall,

1995); *From the Forest to the Sea: A Story of Fallen Trees*, by Chris Maser and others (U.S.D.A. Forest Service, 1988); *Water: A Natural History*, by Alice Outwater (Basic Books, 1996); *The Mammals and Life Zones of Oregon*, by Vernon Bailey (U.S.D.A., 1936); *Reaching Home: Pacific Salmon, Pacific People*, essays by Tom Jay and Brad Matsen (Alaska Northwest, 1994); *The Forest that Fish Built: Salmon, Timber, and People in Willapa Bay*, by Richard Manning (Ecotrust, 1996); and *The Ecology of Running Waters*, by H. B. N. Hynes (Liverpool University, 1970).

In "A Brief History of Eden" I relied heavily on *The Making of Oregon: A Study in Historical Geography*, by Samuel N. and Emily F. Dicken (Oregon Historical Society, 1979). I also gleaned information from *The Willamette Valley: Migration and Settlement on the Oregon Frontier*, by William A. Bowen (University of Washington, 1978); *Environment and Experience: Settlement Culture in Nineteenth-Century Oregon*, by Peter C. Boag (University of California, 1992); *Rivers of the West: A Guide to the Geology and History*, by Elizabeth and William Orr (Eagle Web, 1985); *Oregon: Wet, High, and Dry*, by John O. Dart and Daniel M. Johnson (The Hapi Press, 1981); and essays by Samuel Dicken, Gordon Dodds, and Verne Ray in *The Western Shore: Oregon Country Essays Honoring the American Revolution*, edited by Thomas Vaughn (Oregon Historical Society, 1975).

The Wild and Scenic Rivers of America, by Tim Palmer (Island Press, 1993), was my chief source for

"A Place in the Rivered Land." *These American Lands*, by Dyan Zaslowsky and the Wilderness Society (Holt, 1986), was also useful.

Even with all this good help, I'm sure I've made errors. They belong entirely to me.

I began this work in 1994, when I was the Margery Davis Boyden writing resident at Dutch Henry Ranch in the Rogue River Canyon. I'm grateful to the Boyden clan and to PEN Northwest for that happy privilege.

My thanks to the Knight Library, Science Library, and Oregon Collection of the University of Oregon Library System, and to Fern Ridge Library in Veneta.

I was lured into this project by the beauty of Larry Olson's photographs and by John Laursen's singular record as a book designer. It's been a great pleasure working with them.

And thanks, as always, to Marilyn Matheson Daniel, who keeps finding room for a writer in our life together.

— *John Daniel*

I want to thank my parents, Evelyn Olson and George Olson, for allowing me to become the person I am. Their love and our life in Minnesota among the lakes and rivers helped instill in me a love of nature.

My wife, Colleen Sullivan, deserves much credit for the creation of this book. Over eight years she contributed countless hours of counseling, writing, editing, love, support, and patience. My love goes to you, Colleen, and thank you.

John Laursen's friendship, enthusiasm, advice, and book-making skill have been invaluable. He saw my photographs at the beginning and guided me to the end. I have admired his work for many years, and I am proud to have had him design our book.

I'm grateful to John Daniel for agreeing to write these river essays. His genius has helped make a collection of photographs into a book, and I'm honored to have him as my partner. I can't imagine this book without his participation.

I am very pleased to have worked with John Fielder and his staff at Westcliffe Publishers. John's dedication to the environment and fine art photography have long made me eager to work with him.

Several environmental groups have endorsed this project from the beginning, and I thank them for their commitment. They are the Oregon Natural Resources Council, the Pacific Rivers Council, the Nature Conservancy, and Oregon Trout.

A number of people cared enough about Oregon rivers to contribute to the printing of a book that would be a lasting tribute. Thank you, Doug Nicholson, Duncan Campbell, Jean Vollum, Althea and Sig Halvorson, Dave and Mary Ellen Olson, Al Berreth, Bruce Henderson, Richard Meeker, Richard Humphrey, and Mark Stern.

Several friends acted as auxiliary editors and counselors: Ruth Gundel, Bruce Lellman, Ginny Rosenberg and Mark Stern, and Ann and Steve Seavey.

Demaris Olson, a constant friend, has perpetually encouraged me as an artist.

To the rest of my friends, thanks for your support. Now that the book is finished I look forward to seeing more of you.

— *Larry N. Olson*